D1105514

THE ORIGIN OF DEWEY'S
INSTRUMENTALISM

———

Woodbridge Prize Essay

———

NUMBER FOUR OF THE
COLUMBIA STUDIES IN PHILOSOPHY
EDITED UNDER THE DEPARTMENT OF
PHILOSOPHY, COLUMBIA UNIVERSITY

THE ORIGIN OF DEWEY'S INSTRUMENTALISM

Gabriel

By MORTON G. WHITE

1964
OCTAGON BOOKS, INC.
NEW YORK

Reprinted 1964
by special arrangement with Columbia University Press

OCTAGON BOOKS, INC.
175 FIFTH AVENUE
NEW YORK, N. Y. 10010

LIBRARY OF CONGRESS CATALOG CARD NUMBER: 64-24849

Printed in U.S.A. by
NOBLE OFFSET PRINTERS, INC.
NEW YORK 3, N. Y.

To Lucia

THE WOODBRIDGE PRIZE
IN PHILOSOPHY

The Woodbridge Prize in Philosophy is awarded annually, from the income of the Woodbridge Memorial Fund, for the publication by Columbia University Press of the most deserving research conducted in the Department of Philosophy.

The Woodbridge Memorial Fund was established in 1940 by Professor Frederick James Eugene Woodbridge (1867–1940). During the more than thirty years of his career at Columbia he gave impetus, character, and inspiration to much of the research carried on by his students and colleagues. After his death the Fund was enlarged by a group of his friends, in order to provide also for the endowment of a Woodbridge Memorial Lectureship.

The publication of Dr. White's research marks the first award of the Woodbridge Prize.

ACKNOWLEDGMENTS

I am deeply indebted to Professor Ernest Nagel of Columbia University for many years of stimulating and enlightening philosophical instruction. I also want to thank him and Professor Herbert W. Schneider for their advice and assistance while the manuscript of this book was in preparation. To Professors Irwin Edman, Horace L. Friess, and James Gutmann, of Columbia University, I am grateful for helpful suggestions. My wife has read through every version of the manuscript; whatever poor prose remains in it is my own. I want to thank Professor John Dewey for kindly consenting to answer some of my questions about his past. It should be pointed out, however, that he is responsible neither for my excavations nor for the interpretation I have put upon them.

Grateful acknowledgment is due Columbia University for having granted me a University Fellowship (1940–1941), a William Bayard Cutting Traveling Fellowship (1941–1942), and The Woodbridge Prize in Philosophy (1941–1942)— all of which expedited the writing and publication of this book.

Some passages from *The Philosophy of John Dewey* are quoted by permission of the editors and publishers of *The Library of Living Philosophers,* Northwestern University, Evanston, Illinois.

MORTON G. WHITE

New York
December 1, 1942

CONTENTS

INTRODUCTION   xiii

I.   AMERICAN PHILOSOPHY, 1879   3

II.   GEORGE SYLVESTER MORRIS   12

III.   IDEALISM AND THE NEW PSYCHOLOGY   34

IV.   THE FIRST THREE BOOKS   49

V.   THE LOGIC OF EMPIRICISM   64

VI.   THE LOGIC OF VERIFICATION   79

VII.   FROM ETHICAL IDEALISM TO SOCIAL PSYCHOLOGY   96

VIII.   EVOLUTION AND IDEALISM   109

IX.   EVOLUTION AND ARITHMETIC   126

X.   LOTZE AND INSTRUMENTAL LOGIC   134

XI.   CONCLUSION   149

BIBLIOGRAPHY   153

INDEX   155

INTRODUCTION

The present essay is, in large part, a chronicle of John Dewey's ideas on the nature of inquiry and related subjects. It is therefore a study of an intellectual conversion—Dewey's shift from idealism to instrumentalism. The theme is not a new one. Everyone familiar with Dewey's writings knows that he started his career as an idealist. What is less known, and less discussed, is the effect this early attachment had upon his subsequent logical views.

Lotze, Wundt, Bradley, Green, and Bosanquet were the logicians whose work Dewey praised in his earliest years of philosophical writing. There are no papers in which subtle distinctions are made between them or detailed points in idealist logic discussed. Dewey simply praised them as a school, a school of logicians concerned with the method of scientific thinking. Just as he accepted them wholesale as allies, he grouped his opponents under two banners. First there were the inductive logicians—Mill, Venn, and Jevons —who had the merit of being concerned with the method of science, but the misfortune of being descended from Locke, Berkeley, and Hume. Then there were the formal logicians—Sir William Hamilton and H. L. Mansel— about whom Dewey said nothing complimentary. He scorned their *barbara, celarent* recitations as trivial and useless, and regarded their comments on actual thinking as badly expressed versions of Kant.

Dewey's allegiances and enmities were hardly concealed. They turned up explicitly in his writing on every philo-sophical problem. The opposition to Kant and Hamilton went with opposition to Kantian formalism in all fields.

The critique of inductive logic was associated with his opposition to analytic psychology, utilitarian and hedonistic ethics, and empiricism generally. Both these philosophies—Kantianism and empiricism—were originally rejected on Hegelian grounds. In some special instances Dewey called on outside help; for instance, in attacking empiricist psychology he used the results of the new, experimental psychology. This combination of idealist epistemology and experimental psychology in a common front against empiricism was carried out at length in the *Psychology*, which appeared in 1887. His Hegelian epistemology, which originated under the influence of George S. Morris, was reinforced when he aligned himself with the British neo-Hegelians, especially some of the younger ones, such as Seth, the Haldanes, and Bosanquet. His *Leibniz's New Essays concerning the Human Understanding* (1888) was even more forthright in its idealist organicism and its critique of formalism, dualism, and theories involving a passive mind. The *Outlines of a Critical Theory of Ethics* (1891) was a defense of the ethics of self-realization in the manner of Thomas Hill Green.

The *Outlines* was the last idealist work. In 1892 and 1893 Dewey published two criticisms of Green, in which he broke loose intellectually from the man he had viewed with awe and reverence in 1886. Nevertheless, although idealist theories were disappearing from his writing, idealist language remained. He was saying new things in old ways. It is not surprising, therefore, to find him calling himself an "experimental idealist" in 1894.

Once he had freed himself from the domination of Green and Caird, his interest in evolutionary theory developed rapidly. The concepts of adjustment, tension, and conflict appeared with greater and greater frequency in his writings, and whatever idealist ideas remained were expressed in the sober tones of Darwinian naturalism. For instance, the idealistic belief that norms or standards are never imposed on existence *ab extra* is given new content in his paper "Evolution and Ethics." [1] It is no longer expressed by saying that the real is rational, but rather by a detailed argument to show that ideals themselves arise out of natural situations. Similarly the first essay in the *Studies in Logical Theory* continues this attempt to fill the gap between genesis and value without appealing to Hegelian metaphysics. This desire to locate the standard of thinking within the natural process is, in part, what motivated Dewey's construction of an instrumental logic.

In the present essay I wish to trace the development of Dewey's thought from his earliest work to the *Studies*.

[1] *Monist,* VIII (1898), 321–341.

THE ORIGIN OF DEWEY'S INSTRUMENTALISM

CHAPTER ONE

AMERICAN PHILOSOPHY, 1879

1879, the year John Dewey left the University of Vermont, marked no golden age of American philosophy. It dated the low to which the bone-dry Scottish philosophy of McCosh and the vague speculation of idealism had dragged philosophical thought. Academic philosophy was most handicapped, suffering, in addition to internal injuries, constant supervisory interference. There were, it was estimated at the time by G. Stanley Hall, less than half a dozen colleges and universities where philosophy was entirely freed from reference to theological formulae.[1] "A few," we are told, were "under the personal and perhaps daily supervision of the founders themselves,"[2] who engaged and discharged the members of their faculties as if they were day laborers. The colleges were, on the whole, very poor. A few of them had been established by real-estate companies to help the sale of land; others were always falling under the control of ward-politicians and state legislatures.[3] In short, we may safely say that external circumstances inhibited philosophical inquiry.

The best philosophy available at the time went almost unnoticed. Charles Peirce was totally neglected, and Chauncey Wright, whose posthumous book, *Philosophical Discussions,* represents some of the best pre-Peircean published work in American philosophy, had died prematurely in

---

[1] Hall, "Philosophy in the United States," *Mind,* IV (1879), 89.
[2] *Ibid.,* p. 90.   [3] *Ibid.,* p. 92.

1875. Hall could paint only a gloomy canvas for his British colleagues. In no other country, he thought, were men of high culture tempted "by so many and varied considerations to criticize or instruct rather than to add to the sum of the world's intellectual possessions by doing original work." [4]

Hall's hypothesis to account for the lack of good philosophy also serves to explain the character of the philosophy which was publicly practiced, or better, preached. Many of the "professorings," Hall tells us, were familiar with the writings of the Scottish school: Reid, Stewart, Hamilton, and others. We know, for instance, that H. A. P. Torrey, Dewey's teacher at Vermont, based his teachings on the Scottish philosophy, so that it undoubtedly formed an important part of Dewey's philosophical background. Dewey's references to it in later years almost always contain statements about its functioning as a bulwark of moral and religious beliefs against the dissolving effects of English empiricism. [5] And when he refers to the dissolving effects of English empiricism, he has in mind the empiricism of Alexander Bain, J. S. Mill, and Herbert Spencer, all of whom were being read at the time and attacked by both idealists and Scottish realists as the lineal descendants of Locke, Berkeley, and Hume.

Because of their opposition to this empiricism McCosh regarded the Scottish philosophers as one long line of brave defenders of faith and tradition. By their insistence upon principles "prior to and independent of experience" they served to throw back "the tide of materialism, skepticism, and atheism" and "above all," McCosh urged, they established "certain primary truths as a foundation on which

[4] *Ibid.,* p. 104.
[5] See Dewey's essay "From Absolutism to Experimentalism," in *Contemporary American Philosophy,* Vol. II; also the biographical sketch of Dewey by his daughter, Miss Jane Dewey, in *The Philosophy of John Dewey,* ed. by P. Schilpp (hereafter referred to as "Schilpp").

to rear other truths, and as a breakwater, to resist the assaults of skepticism." [6] With great pride McCosh described the Scottish philosophy as having by patience and shrewdness erected a body of fundamental truth "which can never be shaken, but which shall stand as a bulwark in philosophy, morals, and theology, as long as time endures." [7]

This conception of philosophy as bulwark and breakwater was not peculiar to the American devotees of Scottish philosophy. There was at the time an equally strong tendency in the writings of some Hegelian idealists, particularly those under the influence of English neo-Hegelianism, to stress the intimate relation between philosophy, morals, and theology. George S. Morris, who influenced Dewey's earliest work more than any single man., was a Hegelian and was also concerned to show the fortifying powers of philosophy. The main object of his book *Philosophy and Christianity* (1883) was to demonstrate that "intelligence as such" (and therefore philosophy, the science of "intelligence as such") was the "true bulwark" of religion.[8] Dewey himself, a youthful follower of Morris in 1887, also proclaimed that morals and theology were indissolubly united.[9]

Living in a period when philosophers vied with each other to see who could best preserve the sanctity and stability of religious beliefs, Dewey could not help absorbing this same concern. Although he wrote very little in explicit defense of religion, Dewey had sympathy with the aims of Morris and McCosh. He chose the method of Morris, and later he began the study of T. H. Green and Edward Caird. In 1889 he favorably described Green's main purpose as the reconciliation of science and religion, which, Dewey says, Green achieved by finding one spiritual

[6] McCosh, *The Scottish Philosophy*, pp. 6, 9.   [7] *Ibid.*, p. 11.
[8] *Philosophy and Christianity*, p. vii.
[9] See Dewey's paper "Ethics and Physical Science," *Andover Review,* VII (1887), 573.

principle at the basis of science, ordinary experience, ethics, and religion.[10] One year later, after calling Edward Caird's *The Critical Philosophy of Immanuel Kant* the best book on philosophy in the English language, he praises it specifically for showing that nature is only a factor in "the self-determination of spirit" and for thereby solving "one of the most pressing of contemporary problems." The solution Dewey found so relieving was that "the categories of physical science can be reconciled with the principles of the moral and religious life by being taken up into them." [11]

It would be difficult to maintain that the early Dewey was concerned only with reconciling religion and science. Nevertheless this interest predominates in some of his writings, and the ardor with which he took up Green, Caird and Morris, is partially explained by it. On the other hand there was always the interest in epistemological problems for their own sake, the desire to find out the nature of mind, truth, and knowledge.

The country was not completely parched philosophically in 1879. An occasional oasis appeared. Perhaps the most fortunate thing for Dewey's development was that he decided to study at one of these oases—Johns Hopkins. Although Scottish realism was the most widely taught philosophy in the country, the department of philosophy at Johns Hopkins incorporated every twist of American thought in opposition to the "realism" of McCosh. Its members, at the time, were Charles Peirce, G. S. Morris, and G. Stanley Hall.

Johns Hopkins had been founded in 1876 under the presidency of Daniel Coit Gilman. It was the first university in America to emphasize the importance of graduate study and deliberately set out to attract the people who

10 "The Philosophy of Thomas Hill Green," *Andover Review*, XI (1889), 339.
11 See Dewey's review of Caird's book, *Andover Review*, XIII (1890), 327.

had been running in streams to Germany for their doctor's degrees. With this in mind Gilman proceeded to load his staff with stars and to emphasize the value of seminar work. There seems to have been only one subject to which Gilman lent no great amount of aid; all the available evidence points to the fact that Gilman was an ardent anti-metaphysician. Dewey's biographer tells us [12] that he tried to dissuade Dewey from studying philosophy. R. M. Wenley, in his book on George S. Morris,[13] furnishes us with even more striking evidence of Gilman's anti-speculative direction. But despite this animus (or perhaps because of it), the choice of Peirce, Morris, and Hall as members of the philosophy department, was remarkable when compared with choices made at other universities during the same period. Peirce's greatness becomes more evident as more of his works are read. Hall founded the first laboratory for experimental psychology in America. And Morris—the man people know least about today—was the teacher who had the greatest influence on Dewey. Morris' primary interest was the history of philosophy. He had translated Ueberweg's *History of Philosophy* and had previously studied in Germany, with Ulrici and Trendelenburg. The force of Morris' impact on Dewey is striking. First as a teacher and then as a colleague at Michigan, he helped shape the first fifteen years of Dewey's philosophical thought.

In retrospect this almost total attachment to Morris among the philosophical faculty at Johns Hopkins can very well be regarded as unfortunate. For Peirce had already formulated the outlines of a position which Dewey came to regard as brilliant—but Dewey's discovery of Peirce came twenty years later. Dewey seems to have regarded Peirce as entirely devoted to formal logic. Now it

[12] Schilpp, p. 16.
[13] *The Life and Work of George Sylvester Morris*, pp. 147–155.

is true that Peirce was concerned with formal logic, but it cannot be said that he was a student of formal logic only. For by the time Dewey had come to Johns Hopkins, Peirce had published his papers on pragmatism—"How to Make Our Ideas Clear" and "The Fixation of Belief." [14] The outline of Peirce's course on logic at Johns Hopkins in 1882 [15] shows, provided Peirce followed his announcement even slightly, that at that time he was more than a formal logician. If Dewey was not attracted to Peirce, it was due in great measure to Dewey's Hegelian prejudices against formal logic, even where formal logic was used to solve problems in epistemology. This bias comes out clearly in the last chapter of Dewey's book on Leibniz, written in 1888, while still under Morris' influence.

Although Peirce had no influence on Dewey in these early years, Hall did. Hall was a disciple of Wundt and a hard-headed man who had great contempt for Hegelian speculation. He shared the contempt for Hegel that James expressed in his paper on Hegelisms. In fact, in 1878 Hall himself published a paper in the *Journal of Speculative Philosophy* in which he damned Hegel's method as worthless. This, taken with his high estimate of Peirce, shows how he might have served as an antidote to the bad effects of Hegelianism. Hall's lectures seem to have led Dewey to study experimental psychology. The emphasis is upon the word "study," for Dewey never really became an experimental psychologist in the way other students of Hall did. However, intensive reading brought a wealth of information concerning the latest work in physiological psychology

---

[14] Dewey, in his essay, "The Development of American Pragmatism," says quite correctly, "The articles which Peirce wrote in 1878 commanded almost no attention from philosophical circles, which were then under the dominating influence of the neo-Kantian idealism of Green, of Caird, and of the Oxford School, excepting those circles in which the Scottish philosophy of common sense maintained its supremacy." *Philosophy and Civilization*, pp. 16–17.

[15] See *Journal of Speculative Philosophy*, XVI (1882), 430.

and psychophysics. Dewey's *Psychology*, which appeared in 1887, testifies to the impact of Hall's teaching, but it also evidences Morris' influence. The *Psychology* was a valiant attempt to retain as much of Hegel and neo-Hegelianism as could be retained by one who extolled the "new psychology." In a review [16] of the book Hall attacks Dewey for his attempt to impose Hegelian dogma upon the facts of experimental psychology—presumably the facts to which he led Dewey, which he found utterly incompatible with the idealist speculations of Hegel, Morris, Green, and Caird.

We have before us a picture of Dewey coming to Johns Hopkins in 1882, studying under teachers who expounded absolute idealism, experimental psychology, formal logic, and the philosophy of science. At that time Dewey sided with Morris, the idealist, who had nothing but contempt for the last three disciplines mentioned. This apathy [17] toward the more progressive, scientific tendencies on the campus seems to have brought Morris into conflict with Gilman and to have led to his ultimately leaving Johns Hopkins. His biographer, Wenley, presents some interesting details concerning this rift.[18] Morris realized that the administration did not regard philosophy as something to be petted and encouraged. It gave philosophy none of the support it gave to the experimental sciences. In 1884 it even discontinued the Metaphysical Club, which Morris and Peirce had led at different times. Wenley quotes a letter which indicates that this attack on philosophy was even occurring within the department of philosophy, where it expressed itself as a dispute between Hall and Morris

---

[16] See *American Journal of Psychology*, I (Nov., 1887), 146–164.

[17] Wenley tells us that Morris "was in strong reaction against the 'realistic' tendencies that dominated the university alike in its scientific and humanistic studies" and also that "he literally abominated the current 'philosophy of science'; and the young lions of history, politics and economics, who followed an occasional seminar with him" (p. 151).

[18] *Ibid.*, pp. 147 ff.

over the brand of philosophy they each practiced. The letter is written by Hall to Wenley and records, retrospectively, relations within the philosophy department. Evidently Hall and Morris had known each other for several years before they met at Hopkins. When they first came together there, they saw each other frequently, but soon a change of relations set in. Hall says:

He [Morris] had developed a good way towards the Hegelian position, which his writings illustrated, and so we did not agree. I always felt that his philosophical opinions were so much a part and an expression of his personality, that one could hardly differ from them without danger of losing a little of the warmth of his friendship, and I always felt that his cordiality toward me, although he did not allow it to lapse, consciously faded.

But this was a purely personal matter. Of much greater significance to us are Hall's remarks at the conclusion of his letter:

I think we were both in a sense on trial for a chair at Hopkins; and, when the spirit of the university decided for my experimental type, instead of for the history of philosophy, I always felt that our friendly relations were at an end.[19]

The decision to support Hall's "experimental type" of work as opposed to Morris' was made sometime in 1885. For it was after that date that philosophy became secondary to psychology and pedagogics at Hopkins.[20] The decision was even more dramatically marked, since it was simultaneous with Morris' departure. He left Baltimore at the end of the first semester of 1884–1885, to return to the University of Michigan. It is extremely important to observe that Dewey left Baltimore at almost the same time. For in July, 1884, Dewey was also appointed to the philosophy department at Michigan; it was there that Morris con-

19 *Ibid.*, p. 153.
20 See Wenley, *The Life and Work of George Sylvester Morris*, p. 150.

tinued to influence Dewey, no longer as a teacher, but as a colleague.

As we have already observed, Peirce exerted no influence whatsoever on Dewey in the earliest years of Dewey's development. Yet in 1938 Dewey commented:

The readers who are acquainted with the logical writings of Peirce will note my great indebtedness to him in the general position taken. As far as I am aware, he was the first writer on logic to make inquiry and its methods the primary and ultimate source of logical subject-matter.[21]

What is most significant is that Dewey's earliest conception of logic did not come from Peirce. His earliest years were spent in the coils of a theory of logic which Peirce was condemning even then. Furthermore, although Dewey came to the same general position as did Peirce, it cannot be said that he ever gave himself to painstaking inquiry into scientific inquiry in the manner of Peirce. How then did he come to pragmatism? The route was more devious. We must trace it from its beginnings in the writings of Morris.

[21] *Logic,* p. 9n.

CHAPTER TWO

GEORGE SYLVESTER MORRIS

George Sylvester Morris was born in 1840 and died in 1889.[1] In 1878, after having taught at the University of Michigan, he was appointed part-time lecturer on the history of philosophy and ethics at Johns Hopkins. His major work— from a contemporary point of view—was his translation of Ueberweg's history of philosophy. His other books, those which played a more important role in the development of his students, were: *British Thought and Thinkers* (1880), *Kant's Critique of Pure Reason* (1882), *Hegel's Philosophy of the State and of History* (1887). These works indicate his wholly historical direction. His primary concern was the critical and biographical discussion of major figures in the history of philosophy. For this reason his greatest effect upon Dewey, apart from directing him to a study of the history of philosophy, was to predispose him to certain brands of philosophy—to provide him with allegiances and antagonisms. Morris had a deep-seated preference for German thought and a rabid dislike of British thought before Green. The result for Dewey's earliest philosophical work was crucial. It shaped in a specific way the tenor of approximately the first fifteen years of his work, to say nothing of its general effect on all his later philosophy.

Dewey tells us of Morris' influence in several places. In his article "From Absolutism to Experimentalism" [2] he

---

[1] I am indebted to Wenley, *The Life and Work of George Sylvester Morris,* for the details of Morris' life.

[2] *Contemporary American Philosophy,* ed. by Montague, II, 18.

points out that Morris led him to Hegel. But Morris was not the only force urging him in this direction. The strong British idealist movement of the eighties and nineties, a "reaction against atomic individualism and sensationalist empiricism" had a similar effect. Its elders were the Cairds; some of the younger devotees were Andrew Seth (Pringle-Pattison later), Bernard Bosanquet, and the Haldanes, all of whom contributed to the volume *Essays in Philosophical Criticism* (1883).

This movement [Dewey says] was at the time the vital and constructive one in philosophy. Naturally its influence fell in with and reinforced that of Professor Morris. There was but one marked difference, and that, I think, was in favor of Mr. Morris. He came to Kant through Hegel instead of to Hegel by way of Kant, so that his attitude toward Kant was the one expressed by Hegel himself.[3]

Morris' influence, put in terms of the history of philosophy, was clear in outline at least. He opposed British empiricism and was an ardent supporter of German idealism and what he regarded as its Greek ancestor. Within German idealism he made one fundamental distinction—he preferred Hegel to Kant.

One of Morris' most influential courses was that on the history of philosophy in Great Britain. One of the texts was Green's *Introduction* to Hume, the most powerful critique of empiricism ever written in England. The other text was Morris' own book, *British Thought and Thinkers,* perhaps the sharpest attack on empiricism ever written in America up to that time. The latter is a "biographical, critical and philosophical" consideration of British thought, discussing every important British philosopher from Scotus Erigena to Herbert Spencer. The British are charged, in general, with subordination of theory to practice, skepticism concerning ultimate philosophical questions, and undue elevation of the method of physical science.[4] The net result, according to Morris, was a degenerate neglect of Absolute Spirit. The British refused to study its nature, contenting themselves with religion and science as the only forms of speculation. The result of this, in turn, was a conception of philosophy as worthless metaphysical jargon. Throughout the book the bitter attack on the British lack of philosophy continues. Only one hope is held out for them—they write good verse. This is the "pledge of their speculative ability." With the greatest of scorn Morris gives the British their philosophical due by calling Shakespeare, Wordsworth, Coleridge, and Tennyson their greatest philosophers.

These charges furnish only the emotional trappings of Morris' antagonism. Dewey absorbed very little of this. But Morris carries on more than an emotional attack; he very quickly leaps into the mechanics of English philosophy and proceeds to pick it to bits. These are the sections which had considerable effect on his young pupil.

The treatment of Bacon is the one to be expected. Morris emphasizes and disparages the wax-tablet theory of mind, the belief that we must place the mind in a "purely receptive attitude with reference to nature." He repeats the charges (well-worn even then) concerning Bacon's ineptness at science. The unfortunate attitude toward Copernican astronomy, the failure to see the merits of Gilbert's work, and the remark about his writing science like a Lord Chancellor—all are trotted out in the discussion of Bacon.

Bacon's place in the history of philosophy is easily stated [says Morris]. Of philosophy as such, in distinction from physical science, he had but slight conception and still lighter opinion. For the great truths of ethics, which it is one of the most important works of philosophy to investigate and demonstrate, Bacon was content simply (though honestly enough) to have recourse to "faith," or else let "suffrage decide" . . . Bacon's

4 *British Thought and Thinkers*, p. 36; hereafter referred to as "BTT."

tendency . . . is to make physical science and its method co-extensive with the realm of all knowledge and all method. Physical science is in his view the mother and type of all sciences, and he expressly recommends the application of its method to all subjects—the best (or worst) result of which (as far as it concerns topics ordinarily deemed philosophical or akin to philosophy) is seen in modern descriptive, empirical psychology, and the mechanistic, eudaemonistic (or, in its last result, pessimistic) ethics, founded exclusively upon it.[5]

Hobbes is dispensed with similarly. Morris takes the total effect of his mechanistic argument to be a dismissal of philosophy as an autonomous pursuit. For on Hobbes' view "physical science of phenomena is to take the place of philosophical science of ideal and absolute reality." [6]

The chapters on Locke, Berkeley, and Hume are crucial, particularly the one on Locke. For it is here that Morris gives vent to his feelings on the British theory of mind, the identification of empirical psychology and philosophy; it is here that he delivers a counterattack on those who would dispense with the theory of innate ideas. Each of these discussions had tremendous effect on Dewey. They not only furnished the foundation for his attacks on "the spectator theory of knowledge," but also raised a problem which continued to trouble him for many years—the problem of the relation between psychology and philosophy.

This last question elicits a definite, if not obviously clear statement on Morris' part. He begins with a consideration of J. Croom Robertson's statement that "the most characteristically English movement within modern mental philosophy is the continuous pursuit of psychological inquiry in the spirit of positive science" (*Mind*, January, 1879, quoted in BTT, p. 171). Morris urges that this "psychological inquiry" is *empirical* psychology and is no more entitled to be called "philosophy" (even "mental philosophy") than is physiology or the anatomy of the

5 BTT, pp. 136–137.   6 BTT, p. 167.

brain. Its major task, he says, is "the analysis and classification of mental phenomena." Consequently, "it does not solve any philosophical question concerning cause, substance and purpose." [7] The distinction between empirical and rational psychology, Morris tells us, must be kept clear. The first is an extremely interesting and practically useful "science of phenomena," and knowledge of it is essential to the pursuit of philosophy. The second, which treats of the soul "as an entity, a variously self-manifesting power, and a purpose which it is itself to realize" *is* a portion of philosophy.[8] Empirical psychology deals with phenomena or appearances, whereas rational psychology deals with noumena or realities. The fate of the practitioners of empirical psychology is sealed; they are not philosophers. The conclusion, left unsaid, is nevertheless clear. Locke, who said some interesting and useful things, is not a philosopher.

However, had Locke only admitted that he was making no philosophical contribution, there would have been no quarrel with him. Had he stuck to the purpose ascribed to him by Fox Bourne,[9] there would have been no ground for a lengthy attack, says Morris, patronizingly. But unfortunately, Morris sighs, this was not the case. If only because

In general, those who scout metaphysics are the most dogmatic in their metaphysical assumptions. . . . Every man must have, and does have, consciously or virtually, his philosophy, and if from prejudice, or indolence he will not take it from philosophers, or seek it by appropriate philosophical methods, he is sure to seek it from some other source, and the chances are ten to one that he will be led astray. The empirical psychologist is

---

[7] BTT, p. 171.   [8] BTT, p. 172.

[9] Fox Bourne, Locke's biographer, had said that Locke's aim was "not to build up a metaphysical theory, but to ascertain by actual observation what were the means and methods by which ordinary people acquired knowledge and developed their thinking faculties." Quoted in BTT, p. 192.

rarely content to be that and nothing else, but is prone to seek in his science the answer to philosophical questions.[10]

Locke had had the temerity to question the hypothesis of innate ideas.[11] And on the basis of empirical psychology! Morris is shocked.

Before he begins his critique of Locke, Morris briefly summarizes Locke's attack on innate ideas. And then he points out how Locke's objections to Leibniz's theory are themselves based on a *"static* view of mind and knowledge."[12] Since the mind possesses no power of its own, it is assumed that all the materials of its knowledge come to it by processes which are independent of its own activity. From this it follows, according to Morris, that Locke could not help coming to an incorrect conception of innate ideas. Locke opposed the doctrine of innate ideas because he interpreted it as maintaining that "certain ideas are clearly and necessarily in the mind of every individual from the beginning of his conscious life."[13] Now, since children, savages, idiots, and others are not conscious of such necessary or innate ideas as God, soul, substance, or of innate truths like "Whatever is, is," Locke might very well have concluded, as he did, that there were no such ideas.[14]

But, Morris insists, the notion of innate ideas which permits Locke to dismiss them so easily is the result of a complete misunderstanding of Leibniz. What Leibniz did intend, Morris tries to say, but his explanation is not very clear. His words are:

It [the theory of innate ideas] implies that the mind has a nature and an activity peculiar to itself, for the development of

---

[10] BTT, p. 193.

[11] In connection with this and what follows, see Dewey's book on Leibniz, in which the Locke-Leibniz debate is discussed and where Dewey defends the theory of innate ideas in the manner of Morris. This book of Dewey's is considered below, p. 60.

[12] BTT, p. 194.   [13] BTT, p. 195.   [14] *Ibid.,* p. 195.

which exciting conditions—be these sensible "impressions" or something else may be needed, but which are distinguished in reality, and must be carefully kept distinct in theory from the conditions as such. It implies that mind is not simply and characteristically what it *has*, but what it *does*, not a state, but an activity. "Innate ideas" (an unfortunate phrase, it must be confessed) are the inherent, independent, rational fibres of the mind's own activity (as distinguished from that side of mind by which, as in sensation, it is relatively passive) and it is by no means necessary that they should become visible, and be explicitly and universally and constantly recognized as threads or states of empirical consciousness (or as "ideas"), in order to prove their reality. They are present still, if only virtually and unconsciously, determining the direction and shaping the results of thought, and without them no rational consciousness whatever would be possible.[15]

Even Locke was forced to abandon a completely passive mind, since he endowed it with "powers" and the capacity to operate. Here, Morris says, Locke was "on the track of a conception of mind as an ideal value, a living power, an energy of intelligence." [16] Had he followed this path more carefully, he would have been forced to recognize the existence of powers like Aristotle's active reason or Kant's pure reason.[17] Unfortunately, Morris says, this direction does not prevail in Locke.

Readers even barely familiar with Dewey's later writings on mind cannot help recognizing their similarity to Morris' remarks on the same subject. This kind of attack on passivity is surely the ancestor of Dewey's long crusade against the spectator theory of knowledge. Were we merely interested in the general origin, we might stop here. But it is of considerable interest to fill in the intervening steps, to show in greater detail the impact of idealism on Dewey. The story is not simply a story of his taking over idealism intact, but as we know, a tale of transformation, revision, and overhauling. Dewey is not an idealist, he is what an

[15] BTT, pp. 195–196.   [16] *Ibid.*, p. 196.   [17] *Ibid.*, p. 197.

idealist becomes when he incorporates the results of modern biology, psychology, and social science.

Morris subjects Berkeley and Hume to attacks no softer than those he leveled against Locke. The chapter on Hume is the occasion for contrasting the traditional British conception of consciousness and that held by Morris and his idealist allies. It is couched in difficult, metaphorical language, and is not so much a detailed analysis as an expression almost of temperamental choice. This does not reduce its value for us. On the contrary, it makes us aware of the fervor with which Morris held his views and of the considerable emotional effect he must have had on Dewey. Because Dewey, as we shall see later, orated on the virtues of *dynamic, living* philosophy. Morris says:

The consciousness contemplated by empirical psychology is static, spectacular, sensible.

This is the inanimate hull, not the living kernel of real consciousness, which is dynamic, dramatic, rational. The former is and must be contemplated essentially as a succession of lifeless images or pictures; the latter is vital, self-illuminating, rational activity. The elements of the former are "states of consciousness," passive "feelings," while those of the latter are *acts*. The former are opaque "impressions" which reveal no objective reality that produces and no subjective reality that receives or perceives them. The latter are translucent with the light of self-conscious, active reason. The former are sensible, the latter intelligible. The former are observed, the latter are, in the fullest, deepest sense of the word, experienced; for here act and self-conscious agent are inseparable.[18]

The remainder of *British Thought and Thinkers* is devoted to the three great British philosophers of the nineteenth century—Sir William Hamilton, John Stuart Mill, and Herbert Spencer. Any study of American philosophy during Morris' lifetime must probe deeply into prevailing attitudes toward these three thinkers. All of them figure

---

[18] BTT, p. 255.

in the early thought of Dewey. He labeled Hamilton a "formalist" enemy; he believed that Mill was on the right track as a student of scientific method, but that he was handicapped by his father's psychology. Dewey reacted against Spencer in his earliest years, but was forced by him to consider the problems raised by evolutionary theory. Many of Dewey's earliest opinions of these men find their sources in Morris' writings. Dewey shared Morris' fundamental opposition to all of them. He pared, trimmed, and qualified these first judgments in later years, but the initial impact was of inestimable significance; remnants of it never disappeared.

Morris' examination of Hamilton begins with a discussion of Kant, of whom Hamilton was a follower. It was Kant who captured Morris, and so he spends much time expounding his virtues and defects. Kant admitted only *phenomena,* and these corresponded to Hume's impressions. Kant, Morris says, held that "the order of the concatenation of phenomena" in our knowledge was not arbitrary. It was fixed and necessary. Although, according to Kant, our knowledge presupposes sensible experience, Morris points out that Kant had argued that "a critical analysis of the conditions upon which alone experience is possible, shows that there are known and predetermined forms which it must assume, or grooves in which it must run." These forms, according to Morris' account of Kant,

known or cognizable, *a priori* as necessary and universal, are the mechanism of mind, independent of experience, but useless and without significance, except as applied to the material of knowledge furnished in experience. . . . These forms, "spontaneous functions of the mind," "categories of the understanding," or "ideas of pure reason," . . . are works of the dynamic, vital consciousness, which is the real organ of philosophy, as indeed of all real knowledge.[19]

19 BTT, pp. 290–291.

The critique of Kant is made next. Morris is quick to find errors in proportion to the amount of British psychology at the base of Kant's system. For instance, Kant is said to share "in the constitutional intellectual infirmity, or scientific prejudice of his century, in being unable to see in anything but sensible consciousness a possible type or standard of reality." [20] Because reality is inaccessible to sense, Kant was forced to postulate a thing-in-itself. This leads Morris to say, with bitter sarcasm,

Real being, therefore, which empirical psychology, in spite of its own demonstration that it cannot be an object of sensible perception, still pertinaciously conceives as if it might be an object of such perception if only our senses were superhumanly quickened, becomes merely a mysterious object of unintelligent persuasion or belief, an alleged "thing-in-itself" . . . but in reality, the purest nonsense, a veritable hodge-podge of contradictions. This is the valuable (?) [sic] contribution to his philosophy which Kant received from his study of British psychology.[21]

Morris calls this result "ontological negativism." First we are told, he says, that the mind is not a *tabula rasa,* that it has an independent nature of its own and is capable of activity. And this, from Morris' point of view, is, of course, fine. But then we are told

that mind and all its forms of thought are without "sensuous feeling," empty and unsubstantial, a mask, a spectre. They are somewhat mythically described as having only "logical," not real or ontological, value and significance. Mind is something and it is nothing. It is the all-efficient determining factor with reference to the form of knowledge, but it is a factor whose own substance and reality are reduced to the mere shadow of a "point of view." All this absurdity and jargon result simply from the potent spell of the sensuous prejudice above noted.[22]

Of course, Kant is not completely condemned. For at the end of his discussion Morris takes time to state his

[20] BTT, p. 291.   [21] BTT, pp. 291–292.   [22] BTT, p. 292.

virtues, to indicate the progressive elements in Kant's philosophy. His very recognition of forms and functions of mind which were not sensuous "showed that he was also under another spell—the spell of vital, absolute reality." [23] Kant's demonstration of these forms in the most ordinary phases of experience was for Morris a demonstration of the power and reality of the "energy of intelligence." And this, according to Morris, was an "ideal activity, not a merely passive state of conscious feeling, but self-conscious spiritual *doing,* or dynamic self-consciousness." [24] Kant, we see, was a critical point. He marks the beginning of German idealism, but not the crowning point. For this we must wait for Hegel. Nevertheless the active mind is here to stay. All future contributions to philosophy must begin with this as prolegomenon. So it is with Dewey. Here is the first major historical antecedent of Dewey's activism. It is not *identical* with Dewey's activism, and it must be emphasized that Dewey revises this doctrine considerably. Nowhere, for instance, in Morris' discussion of the active mind do we find a reference to bodily activity. On the basis of Dewey's own later distinction between pure *activity* and practical, bodily *action,*[25] one might say that Morris emphasized the former, but never in his analysis of knowledge came to recognize the importance of the latter.

As yet we have not come to the main theme of this chapter in Morris' book—the philosophy of Sir William Hamilton. And for a very obvious reason. Morris is much more excited by Kant, and so his discussion of him, even though preparatory to the one of Hamilton, is of considerable length. For Morris, Hamilton was a rather poor edition of Kant. The comments on him are brief. We cannot help feeling that they are partially responsible for Dewey's re-

23 *Ibid.,* p. 292.   24 BTT, p. 293.
25 *The Quest for Certainty,* pp. 17–19.

mark in 1890, that "Mansel and Hamilton had indeed presented a Kant of whom the less said the better." [26]

Hamilton was not only a disciple of Kant, but also a disciple of Reid.

Under Kantian inspiration he develops, in forms of sharp outline, the self-confessed, yet comparatively unobtrusive, theoretical agnosticism of Reid. Under the influence of Reid and of British psychological method, he emasculates the element of virile idealism, which was in Kant.[27]

He absorbs the empiricism of both his teachers. That is, he sets up "sensible consciousness" as "the Bible of philosophy," so that the "ultimately real" becomes unknowable for us. "All our knowledge is relative, being confined to conditioned existence . . . in time and space." [28] Morris then remarks parenthetically that Hamilton's substitution of his three categories—conditioned existence, time, and space—for Kant's forms of sensibility and categories of the understanding, was a step in the wrong direction. In tendency Hamilton thus "eliminates the dynamic element from Kant, as an empirical psychologist would be likely to do." [29]

The treatment of John Stuart Mill follows that of Hamilton. It indicates very clearly that Morris did not accept the Mill-Hamilton controversy as exhausting all possible positions in philosophy. It must be remembered that he was attacking British thought, not simply English thought. So far as he was concerned, both Mill and Hamilton were foolishly bound to the vicious consequences of accepting psychology as philosophy. The immediate tradition behind Mill is dragged over very glowing coals; no bit of invective is held back in the discussion of James Mill and Bentham. Using the fact that *British Thought and Thinkers* is partially biographical, Morris takes time to quote

---

[26] *Andover Review*, XIII (1890), 328.
[28] BTT, p. 295.
[27] BTT, p. 294.
[29] *Ibid.*, p. 295.

Bain's comment on the elder Mill: "The one disagreeable trait in Mill's character, and the thing that has left the most painful memories, was the way that he allowed himself to speak and behave to his wife and children before visitors." [30] This, in conjunction with the elder Mill's education of John, is taken as evidence of a correlation between his cruelty and, apparently, his failure to be an idealist. Morris devotes many pages to attacking the drill method of John Stuart's education. In the same vein Jeremy Bentham is dismissed as "a Philistine à outrance," who thought that all that mankind needed to know, and all they were really able to know was on what side their bread was buttered.[31] As might be expected, the well-known crisis in Mill's life is capitalized upon as showing the inadequacy of the world-view bequeathed him. With considerable delight in confirming a pet hypothesis, Morris adds "that it was precisely from Wordsworth, the poet-philosopher of mind directly opposite to that in which he had been brought up," that Mill derived greatest comfort and spiritual furtherance in later years.[32]

Finished with this excursus into personalia, Morris returns to hammer away on a familiar theme. "Mill's philosophy is nothing but empirical psychology, arbitrarily universalized and put, to its own injury, in the place of philosophy." [33] According to it, Morris says,

All knowledge is made intensely subjective, individual, being confined to particular states of consciousness, and to the actually observed, but, by express declaration, not necessary, and otherwise unfathomable, order which exists among them. Accordingly, also, no provision is made for thought, as something which, if it, and an organ appropriate to it, exist, is necessarily something other than mere atomic or complex *states* of consciousness. No provision is made for the recognition of any mental *activity* whatsoever, and, such activity being neverthe-

---

[30] See *Mind*, II (1877), 550; also quoted in BTT, p. 312.
[31] BTT, p. 307.   [32] *Ibid.*, p. 324.   [33] *Ibid.*, p. 330.

less presupposed, nothing is left for it to do but to stare at and analyse its own "states." [34]

There remains only one more Briton for Morris to pounce upon—Herbert Spencer. And he pounced upon him with all the savagery he was capable of using on an "empirical psychologist." His purpose in this chapter, he says in the Preface, is to follow the main thought of volume "out of the British past into the immediate present." [35] In this he emulates, as he does continually, Thomas Hill Green, who, on the first page of his essay on Spencer and Lewes, says, "each generation requires the questions of philosophy to be put to it in its own language, and, unless they are so put, will not be at the pains to understand them." [36] Thus Morris turns to the latest version of British empiricism, this time wrapped in the almost deceiving cloak of evolutionary theory, or so Morris will argue. The keynote of the chapter is the fundamental distinction Morris made between philosophy and science. The Spencerian *Unknowable,* Morris maintains, cannot be masqueraded as the assured result of evolutionary biology. On the contrary, he argues, it is simply the product of Spencer's repetition of the words of his British masters. And not only must his philosophy be distinguished from evolutionary biology and empirical psychology—it must be distinguished from all "physical science." Philosophy is the study of absolute spirit, and its methods are completely different from those of science. The greatest error committed by British philosophy according to Morris was its failure to make this distinction. The result is a groping in the dark. British philosophy bears the same relation to true philosophy, according to Morris, as pre-Socratic philosophy bore to Plato and Aristotle.

Morris was so involved, emotionally and intellectually, in his antagonism toward British philosophy and his al-

[34] BTT, pp. 330–331.   [35] *Ibid.,* p. 4.   [36] Green, *Works,* I, 373.

legiance to German philosophy, that he instituted a series of books to spread the truth. The series, "German Philosophic Classics for English Readers and Students," was published by S. C. Griggs & Co., in Chicago. Its first volume, written by Morris, appeared in 1882. It was called *Kant's Critique of Pure Reason*. The Preface quotes part of the prospectus [37] for the series:

Each volume will be devoted to the critical exposition of some one masterpiece belonging to the history of German philosophy. The aim in each case will be to furnish a clear and attractive statement of the special substance and purport of the original author's argument, to interpret and elucidate the same by reference to the historic and acknowledged results of philosophic inquiry, to give an independent estimate of merits and deficiencies, and especially to show, as occasion may require, in what way German thought contains the natural complement, or the much-needed corrective, of British speculation.[38]

Apart from furnishing us with a lengthy statement of Morris' views on Kant, this book, more than the one on British thought, gives us a glimpse of the outlines of Morris' philosophy. It has the added attraction of appearing in the same series as Dewey's *Leibniz's New Essays concerning the Human Understanding*. When we examine Dewey's book we shall observe how Morris influenced Dewey on the British-versus-German issue. Morris' book on Kant makes it easy to understand Dewey's remark that Morris came to Kant through Hegel.[39] Morris' book on Kant concentrates its attack on dualism, whereas the one on British thought was more concerned with destroying theories invoking a passive mind. *British Thought and Thinkers* and *Kant's Critique of Pure Reason*, together,

[37] The prospectus first appeared in *The Journal of Speculative Philosophy* of 1881.
[38] *Kant's Critique of Pure Reason*, pp. v–vi.
[39] See above, p. 13.

supply a wonderful picture of the origins of the two central doctrines of Dewey's instrumentalism, activism, and anti-dualism. To make matters easier, however, the reader may simply examine a paper by Morris, written in 1882, in which he presents a summary of his whole philosophy. He called it "Philosophy and Its Specific Problems." [40]

As the title may suggest, Morris' purpose in this paper was to establish the existence of philosophy as a special study, having specific problems of its own. The first step was to meet those who identified philosophy with what Morris called "physical science." Following Bacon, Morris meant by "physical science," "inquiries into the constitution and modes of action of corporeal objects." Such a conception of philosophy, Morris pointed out, was not new. It stemmed from the pre-Socratics and the Sophists, he said; it was practiced in his day, he was sure, by every British empiricist. As Morris understood the doctrine it maintained that philosophy was simply the set of all "the largest generalizations of physical science." Furthermore, Morris interpreted it as holding that "what is knowable is sensible phenomena, and these are, as more particularly described, phenomena of the 'redistribution of matter and motion.'" Fastening on Spencer's statements, Morris attributes to him the belief that such generalizations afforded the final explanation of all that man could know. Knowledge, intelligence, will, purpose, the pursuit and realization of ideals in society, the state, art, and religion—all these, Morris says—are regarded by his opponents as "knowable only so far as they can be reduced to the phenomena of the redistribution of matter and motion." Briefly, Morris assigns to his opponents the view that all science is physical science and that no other science is possible. And while

[40] *The Princeton Review*, IX (N.S., 1882), 208–252; hereafter the article is referred to as "PSP."

they hold that there is some *absolute reality* distinct from physical objects, they maintain it is *unknowable* and therefore no object of intelligible concern.

With the practice of physical science Morris has no quarrel. In fact he admits that it is a prerequisite, even a handmaiden, to philosophy. His only dispute is with those who regard physical science as exhaustive of all knowledge. In this discussion, of course, we are never told just what the phrase "physical science" means. That is, we are never sure whether it is synonymous with "empirical science," or with "physics." If the first interpretation is correct, then, excluding mathematics and logic, one might easily hold that physical science is exhaustive of all knowledge. But then we would simply be maintaining the mildest empiricist position—namely, that all our knowledge can be confirmed by an appeal to sense experience. On the other hand, if by "physical science" Morris meant "physics" it would be easier to attack the thesis he was attacking. For according to the latter interpretation one would simply have to show that not all true empirical statements could be deduced from the science of physics. It is never clear whether Morris accepts either of these interpretations of "physical science." He himself puts the issue as follows. Philosophy, he says, is "the examination of our whole and undivided experience with a view to ascertaining its whole nature, its range and its content." [41] Knowledge is nothing but the interpretation and comprehension of experience. But what about experience? Morris asks. Is all experience sensible? If it is, then all knowledge is sensible, and nothing, therefore, can be uttered outside the domain of physical science. But clearly, Morris argues, this is not true. There is experience which is not sensible. Consequently there is a discipline which is not included within

[41] "Philosophy and Its Specific Problems," *The Princeton Review*, IX (N.S., 1882), 212.

physical science. Philosophy, in its attempt to study the whole of experience, is that discipline. Moreover, Morris claims that philosophy is capable of experimental verification. He does not allow himself to be labeled an apriorist, who is not interested in testing his statements. On the contrary, he believes his philosophy to be more experimental [42] than any of the empirical philosophies. Why? His answer is his critique of British empiricism.

The fundamental assumption of empiricism, Morris says, is that all our knowledge and experience is sensible. According to this assumption all our knowledge is confined to the consciousness of our own mental states or feelings. It follows that we have no knowledge of the external world or of ourselves as knowing agents. In consequence, empiricists must hold that the self and the external world, if they exist at all, are "meta-physical" entities. In this way both selves and the world are conceived as lying behind or beyond "empirico-sensible" consciousness. But empiricists recognize that we have beliefs in the existence of the external world. How do they explain them? They find them wholly unaccountable, mysterious. Still, British philosophy found itself morally obliged to construct some sort of scientific justification for the beliefs in question.

And so the problem respecting the existence of the external world could become, in the language of Mr. Bain, the "great problem of metaphysics in the eighteenth century," as it still is for Mr. Bain and other metaphysicians, the Mills, Spencers, and their like, of the nineteenth century.[43]

It is upon this concern of British philosophy that Morris visits complete contempt.

[42] The word "experimental" appears throughout the paper. This usage might have influenced Dewey's choice of the word "experimentalism" as a name for his philosophy. Particularly as a means of distinguishing it from British empiricism. See, in this regard, Dewey's "An Empirical Survey of Empiricisms," *Studies in the History of Ideas,* edited by the Department of Philosophy of Columbia University, Vol. III.

[43] PSP, pp. 213-214.

Since all ground of evidence upon which to solve the "problem" is cut away by the dogmatic theory of knowledge or experience adopted at the outset, it follows that all discussion of it, all ostensible weighing of evidence concerning it, can really only consist in a dialectical beating of the air, dancing or trying to dance in an intellectual vacuum, pompously uttering words and phrases which have a solemn sound but convey no meaning.[44]

This charge is repeated throughout Morris' writings. It holds for Hamilton as well as the English philosophers. The point is clear enough. Morris wishes to expose the empiricists and the intuitionists as purveyors of meaningless metaphysics. This is another instance of Morris' plaguing both houses—"empirical" and "intuitional" empiricism. We shall meet both these tendencies in Dewey's writings. He, too, lumps Hamilton and Mill together for certain purposes, and also violently rejects the existence of the external world as a "problem" worth discussing. One of his attacks on Bertrand Russell [45] is directly in the line of Morris' attack on Bain and company.

Morris' criticism of empiricism needs only one more generalization to round it out. The contention finally made is that empiricism is guilty of the worst kind of abstraction: "it mutilates man, tearing the organic whole of his living experience into miserable shreds." [46] Here we have an expression of Morris' Hegelian organicism, one of the most important theses Dewey absorbed in his youth. Put roughly, Morris' assertion was that experience is an organic, living whole, which is rendered lifeless by the

[44] PSP, p. 214.

[45] In 1915 Dewey wrote some comments on Russell's *Our Knowledge of the External World,* called "The Existence of the World as a Logical Problem." They appeared first in *Phil. Review,* XXIV, 357–370, and later in *Essays in Experimental Logic.* In the same year he wrote the following in an appreciation of Morris: "I remember the scorn with which he alluded to Bain's reference to the problem of the existence of the external world as the great problem of metaphysics" (see Wenley, *The Life and Work of George Sylvester Morris,* p. 317).

[46] PSP, p. 215.

dissecting processes of analytic empiricism. Ultimately this dissection is said to lead to dualism, against which Morris savagely inveighs. His anti-dualism was perhaps the first variety adopted by Dewey himself.

British dualism, Morris maintained, isolated two factors in the knowledge-situation—an object to be known and a subject fitted to know. Furthermore, Morris tells us, the relation between subject and object is, according to the dualists, purely mechanical, a matter of impact. Now Morris distinguishes two types of relations, in a typically Hegelian fashion. Some relations he calls "mechanical," others he calls "organic." Two things, he says, stand in a mechanical relation to each other if there is no third living thing of which they are both a part (the term "part" not being clearly defined). Thus the relation between two billiard balls which collide is a mechanical one. On the other hand, two things stand in an organic relation to each other if there is a third living thing which contains both of them as parts. Empirical consciousness, which Morris never defines, is said to stand in an organic relation to the objects of knowledge. This means, of course, that there is some living whole of which they are both "parts." He argues that at first the knowledge relation seems to be a mechanical relation, that is, a relation between human beings and objects. But this is only "appearance." What are related are "consciousnesses" and objects. But these consciousnesses, which are empirical consciousnesses, the consciousnesses of particular men, are different from universal consciousness. Universal consciousness is that third thing which embraces empirical consciousnesses and the objects of knowledge. Since both empirical consciousness and objects are imbedded within this larger, living whole, they partake of a common spirit, or life. Universal consciousness is the living unity stressed throughout Morris' writings. For Dewey it was the most influential concept in his early writings. Here we have not only an epistemological device for unifying the subject and object of knowledge, but a unity which is alleged to exist throughout the world. In social theory this is a particularly important notion, since it stresses the unity of all social action. It is the basis upon which almost any dualism is attacked. And here, perhaps, we have the means for making clear what dualism meant for the early Dewey. It was any doctrine which maintains that two things are mechanically related, when as a matter of fact they are organically related. This stimulated Dewey to hunt for these organic relations throughout his life. First in epistemology; then in biology; then in sociology. In general we shall be concerned with this process of naturalizing idealist doctrines, as it occurs in Dewey's writings.

Our study of Morris should prepare us for following the early work of Dewey. The period dating from 1884 to 1890 is crammed with ideas closely related to those of Morris and other idealists. But one historical point should always be kept in mind. Dewey's attack on dualism, discontinuity, and passivity appeared before he was detailedly occupied with developments in psychology, or Darwinian biology, or modern sociology. He drew directly on Morris, Hegel, and the British neo-Hegelians for his attack on dualism and allied heresies. It is not until his own positive doctrine emerges that he uses the modern developments mentioned. They did appear in his earliest writings, but only incidentally. Then Dewey would most likely have attacked British empiricism with the weapons forged by Hegel and Green and would have regarded confirmation coming from biology as so much extra, but not decisive, evidence on his side. In the beginning the primary emphasis was Hegelian. The continuity between man and nature, which later was a biological concept drawn from the evolutionists, was in the earliest days a continuity within universal consciousness. The activity which later became manual and bodily was, at this early point, a vague, sometimes even mentalistic (in Dewey's sense today) "energy of intelligence."

CHAPTER THREE

IDEALISM AND THE NEW
PSYCHOLOGY

Morris pushed Dewey further and further in the direction
of Hegelian idealism. He prepared him for the work of
Green, Caird, and the young British idealists whose work
appeared in the *Essays in Philosophical Criticism*. But at
the same time Dewey, under the tutelage of Hall, immersed
himself in the literature of the "new psychology." The result of these two interests was a large-scale attempt throughout the eighties to state the relation between idealism and
psychology. Dewey's *Psychology,* which appeared in 1887,
is an expression of these two elements in his thinking. But
even before the *Psychology* appeared he had published
some articles which picture his development clearly. In
1884 two of these appeared, two of the most interesting:
"Kant and Philosophic Method," [1] and "The New Psychology." [2] The first was an expression of his idealism, the
second an eloquent appraisal of the latest developments in
psychology. The first testified his allegiance to Morris,
while the second aligned him with Hall. Thus Dewey was
both the idealist philosopher and the follower of the new
psychology. However, he did not rest easily in both these
positions, for he saw problems that neither side dealt with.
This restlessness was intensified when he began to read
the British idealists, particularly Caird. He was forced to

[1] *Journal of Speculative Philosophy,* XVIII, 162–174.
[2] *Andover Review,* II, 278–289.

discover for himself just what the relation between philosophy and psychology was. Because on the one hand the idealists were bent upon showing that psychology was not philosophy, and on the other, Wundt, the central figure in the new psychology, was claiming that philosophy was nothing but psychology. These counterclaims, made by men he respected, whose doctrines he supposedly followed, left Dewey in a peculiar position. It was this that led him to express himself on the whole question. In 1886 two papers appeared in *Mind*, in which he tried to state his position on the relation between philosophy and psychology. The first was called "The Psychological Standpoint," [3] the second, "Psychology as Philosophic Method." [4]

KANT AND PHILOSOPHIC METHOD

Dewey's 1884 paper on Kant was a Hegelian criticism of Kant. It adds very little to what Morris had said and is directly influenced by Edward Caird and the *Essays in Philosophical Criticism*. Philosophy is said to arise when people feel the need of going deeper into things, when they are no longer content "with haphazard views or opinions derived from this or that science." [5] As a result they begin to search for some principle which, "true on its own account, may also serve to judge the truth of all besides." Philosophy for the early Dewey is explicitly the science which is to provide a truth-criterion. Therefore different philosophies are to be examined for their ability to provide such a criterion. Descartes, British empiricism, and Kant are all paraded before the reader, and their attempts to provide a theory of truth are criticized for failures of one sort or another. This paper typifies the first serious "period" of Dewey's career. Its concern with methodology, its critique of empiricism and Kant, its praise of Hegel—these are all

---

[3] *Mind*, XI, 1–19. [4] *Ibid.*, pp. 153–173.
[5] *Journal of Speculative Philosophy*, XVIII, 162, 166.

marked from the start as coming straight from Morris, Caird, and the young English idealists. The standard idealist position on British empiricism is accepted completely. Empiricism's conception of mind as a blank, a wax tablet, and a *tabula rasa* is strenuously opposed. Since the empiricist criterion of truth involves an analysis of perceptions with agreement as criterion, the mind must be capable of forming these agreements, that is, it must be capable of synthesis. But the empiricists robbed the mind of its active powers. Consequently, Dewey points out, Kant, who turned to empiricism for a truth-criterion in his youth, was sorely disappointed.

Like Morris and Seth Pringle-Pattison,[6] Dewey admits that Kant made an important contribution, but at the same time he does not fail to criticize him. According to Dewey, Kant conceived of thought as active, but also as purely formal or analytic. It was sharply cut off from its material. On one side of the barricade sat active, but formal, thought, preening itself on its energetic, lively nature. On the other side, a hopeless mess, in Dewey's opinion, "a blind rhapsody of particulars, without meaning or connection." The great problem was how to establish contact. Kant, according to Dewey, took the only path. This was to assume "that while thought *in itself* is analytic, it is synthetic when applied to material given it, and that from this material, by its functions, it forms the objects which it knows."[7] Here, Dewey claims, reason and its material are separated; both are taken as foreign to each other. He is willing to admit that the individual is distinct from the materials of his thought, just as Morris did. But, he maintains, this is not to say that "Reason" itself is foreign to these materials. Like Morris' universal consciousness, Dewey's "Reason" is the living unity in which all things participate. It follows

[6] See *Essays in Philosophical Criticism,* p. 11.
[7] *Journal of Speculative Philosophy,* XVIII, 164.

that "the material which was supposed to confront Reason as foreign to it, is but the manifestation of Reason itself." [8] Given both subject and object of knowledge as manifestations of Reason, "we find ourselves forced into the presence of the notion of organic relation." [9] Therefore the relation between subject and object is not external or mechanical, for "the only conception adequate to experience as a whole is organism." Dewey then raises, but does not answer, the question, "What is involved in the notion of organism?" [10]

From the attack on Kant, Dewey goes to the praise of Hegel. Here he finds the corrections which were needed. The first point concerns Hegel's refusal to distinguish sharply between subjective and objective existences. It follows that we can no longer refer to "things and thoughts as two distinct spheres." [11] In Hegel's logic we get an account "of the conceptions or categories of Reason which constitute experience, internal and external, subjective and objective, and an account of them as a system, an organic unity in which each has its own place fixed. It is the completed *Method of Philosophy*." And so it is that Hegel *completes* Kant, whose thought is critical, transitional. In the early Dewey's mind, and perhaps in the older Dewey's mind, Kant represents the "transition of the old abstract thought, the old meaningless conception of experience, into the new concrete thought, the ever growing, ever rich experience." [12]

THE NEW PSYCHOLOGY

In the eighties Dewey's experience was growing. He was closely in touch with psychology and was interested in the new results in biology. Miss Jane Dewey's comments on

---

[8] *Ibid.*, p. 168.   [9] *Ibid.*, p. 169.   [10] *Ibid.*, p. 170.
[11] *Ibid.*, p. 171; also see Green, *Works*, 338, and Seth Pringle-Pattison, *The Development from Kant to Hegel* (1882), p. 5, and Hegel, *Logic*, Wallace's translation, first edition, Sec. 22.
[12] *Journal of Speculative Philosophy*, XVIII, 174.

Dewey's relations with Hall are therefore of interest. Hall, whatever his merits as a psychologist or philosopher, was an ardent propagandist for experimental psychology. Miss Dewey says:

G. Stanley Hall's discursive lectures on psychological topics, experimental and theoretical, had left him [Dewey] with the belief that the relation between psychology and philosophy was an intimate one, but one which must be worked out on the basis of the new experimental psychology. Experiment was overthrowing the older "rational psychology" traditionally associated with philosophy, and probably an ambition to help bring about an alliance of the new psychology with philosophy was directing Dewey's intellectual activity to a greater extent than he realized.[13]

Hall was the teacher of almost the whole first generation of American experimental psychologists. Among his students, he tells us, "were John Dewey, J. Mackeen Cattell, H. H. Donaldson, E. C. Sanford, W. H. Burnham, G. W. T. Patrick, Joseph Jastrow, James H. Hyslop, Y. Motora, E. M. Hartwell . . . M. I. Swift, and J. Nelson."[14] The psychology he taught, he continues,

was almost entirely experimental and covered for the most part the material that Wundt had set forth in the later and larger edition of his *Physiological Psychology*. Here I spent much time in my laboratory, where there were always students engaged upon specific problems of research, some of the first of which were published in *Mind* and most in later years in the early volumes of my *American Journal of Psychology*.[15]

Although Dewey was one of Hall's students he never carried on original research in experimental psychology. At least we have no published results of such research. In his *Psychology*, of course, we see that he took great interest in physiological psychology, and was extremely *au courant* of developments in it. This great concern was first ex-

13 Schilpp, pp. 22–23.
14 Hall, *Life and Confessions of a Psychologist*, p. 232.
15 *Ibid.*, p. 234.

pressed in 1884, when his paper "The New Psychology" [16] appeared. This paper was directed against the analytic psychology of the British school, whose members Dewey labeled as dissectionists, people who cut up experience, and neatly stowed the parts away in pigeonholes. He stressed the complexity of mental life, which British psychology failed to take into account.

Optimism is the keynote of the article. Consequently Dewey urges the reader not to occupy himself solely with attacking this erroneous theory of the mind. British empiricism, he says, served a purpose, and its limitations were the limitations of the age in which it originated. "The best we can do is to thank them [the empiricists], and then go about our *own* work; the worst is to make them the dividing lines of schools, or settle in hostile camps. . . . We are not called upon to attack them for *our* work is in the future." [17]

Turning his attention away from the past errors of analytic psychology, Dewey outlines the characteristics of the new psychology. Its most important characteristic for Dewey, is its experimental direction, its "tireless study of the secrets of nature," its "counting nothing unclean." Its use of physiology as a means of supplementing introspection was an instance of the experimentalism of the new psychology. But physiology was not the only other science it drew upon. It also appealed to the latest developments in psychiatry, the social sciences, and biology.

Biology contributed the concept of organism. Although traces of this concept are to be found, Dewey says, long before the rise of biology as a science, we must recognize, he continues, that "the great role which the 'organic' conception has played of late is doubtless due in great measure to the growth of biology." [18] Here we see the merging of two strains in Dewey's background. On the one hand there

16 *Andover Review*, II, 278–289.   17 *Ibid.*, p. 280.   18 *Ibid.*, p. 285.

was the organicism he got from Hegel, the organicism he expressed in his paper on Kant. On the other, there was his interest in the concept of organism as that was used by biologists. The Hegelian theory of organic relations was, Dewey thought, confirmed by the organismic direction of biology. Later a thoroughgoing Darwinism forces Dewey to surrender Hegel. But it cannot be emphasized too strongly that it was this similarity of approach which Dewey saw between Hegel and biology that paved the way for the second period of Dewey's career. In these earliest writings the concept of organism is put to many uses. First of all it is used to defend and amplify idealism's attack on the empiricist theory of mind. Then it is directed at all faculty psychologies for their atomistic tendencies. Finally, it led Dewey to recognize the importance of the social environment of man. For the notion of organism brought with it the notion of environment, which in turn suggested "the impossibility of considering psychical life as an individual, isolated thing developing in a vacuum." [19] The way in which this organicism ultimately leads to a conception of all psychology as social psychology will appear later as the result of a combination of Hegelian doctrine and biology.

Hegelian doctrine and the new psychology were not only responsible for Dewey's opposition to empiricist psychology. They also served to stir up an opposition to formal logic. One of the most important features of the new psychology, according to Dewey, was "the rejection of a formal logic as its model and test." [20] He accused the older psychologists of having held to a nominalistic logic. They tried

to make living concrete facts square with the supposed norms of an abstract, lifeless thought . . .

They emasculated experience till their logical conceptions could deal with it; they sheared it down till it would fit their logical boxes; they pruned it till it presented a trim tameness which would shock none of their laws; they preyed upon its vitality till it would go into the coffin of their abstractions.

This is one of the first in a long series of tirades against formal logic. It is not until later that such onslaughts become detailed. At that moment they lay smoldering—but unsupported. This distaste for formal logic, Hegelian in origin, is one of the impulses which ultimately leads to the construction of instrumental logic.

By 1884, we may infer from our study of Dewey's papers of that year, Dewey had made clear just what he opposed. As a result of aligning himself with idealism and the new psychology, he had forged weapons for his attacks on empiricism and formalism. As long as it was a question of criticizing formal logic and the empiricist epistemology, his idealism and his psychology could participate in a kind of united front. Against a common enemy they were in smooth harmony. But very soon Dewey met with difficulties. He could not stave off making a decision concerning the two counterclaims mentioned above. Either philosophy was nothing but psychology, or it was an independent, autonomous discipline. He must side either with Wundt or with Edward Caird. This was the first serious problem Dewey ever considered in print. It was the main concern of his first articles in *Mind*.

PHILOSOPHY AND PSYCHOLOGY

The articles which appeared in *Mind* in 1886 were heavily laden with what Dewey had learned from Thomas Hill Green, "of whom the writer [Dewey] would not speak without expressing his deep, almost reverential attitude." From an idealist point of view—the view Green had defended so arduously—to accept the identity of philosophy and psychology was to follow directly in the footsteps of British empiricism. And Dewey, as we have seen, had just as low an opinion of empiricist epistemology as any idealist. Therefore any attempt on Dewey's part to defend the thesis that philosophy was psychology had to be qualified in some way, so as to help Dewey escape the epithet "empiricist." In his first paper, "The Psychological Standpoint," he accomplishes this delicate task by saying that both British empiricism and British idealism use the psychological method, only idealism used good psychology, while empiricism used bad psychology. The empiricists began with a correct psychological approach, but soon abandoned it. The idealists, on the contrary, continued the very tradition which Locke began, but which Locke himself, Hume, and Berkeley all deserted.

In his first paper Dewey tries to formulate the meaning of the phrase "psychological standpoint." He says that Locke defined this standpoint when he argued that the nature of all objects of philosophic inquiry was to be fixed by finding out what experience said about them. But because Locke introduced his unknowables—mind and matter—he left the psychological standpoint. Berkeley, too, "deserted the method in his reference of ideas to a purely transcendent spirit." [21] And Hume? Hume was the most difficult to prove a deserter. For he was the traditional picture of someone safely planted on psychological ground. But even Hume will be found guilty, Dewey says, if one looks closely. Instead of determining the nature of objects by an appeal to experience, Hume reversed the procedure. "He started with a theory as to the nature of reality and determined experience from that. The only reals for him were certain irrelated sensations and out of these knowledge arises or becomes." [22] But if knowledge comes after them, they can never be known. The conclusion is that Hume, just as much as Locke, assumes that something unknowable exists.

[21] "The Psychological Standpoint," *Mind*, XI, 3.   [22] *Ibid.*, p. 3.

Dewey believed that the "bare sensation," which Hume regarded as the origin of knowledge, was simply a version of Kant's "thing-in-itself." Because, he argued, this sensation is either known or it is not known. If it is known, he maintained, it cannot be said to precede knowledge. If it is not known, it is an unverifiable object, and hence no good psychologist can refer to it without shame. Armed with this bit of dialectic, Dewey challenges the reader to find a point in his own life-history when he had no knowledge. The first objector constructed by Dewey answers by saying that there was a point when he had sensations and when he had no knowledge, but that a little later in his life he began to know. Dewey replies that these infantile sensations are not unknown, because, obviously, his informant knows about them the moment he refers to them. But then the objector becomes more persistent, and says: "I know about them *now* in so far as I am talking about them, but I did not know about them *then,* in my infancy." It is in his answer to this objector that Dewey is forced to bring in the idealist notion of a universal consciousness.

Dewey says:

The fact that sensations exist before knowledge and that knowledge comes about by their organic registration is undisputed . . . An infant . . . is . . . a known object existing in the world of experience; and his nervous organism and the objects which affect it . . . are known objects. . . . Surely it is not a baby thing-in-itself which is affected, nor a world thing-in-itself which calls forth the sensation. It is the known baby and a known world in definite action and reaction upon each other, and this definite relation is precisely a sensation . . . But such a relation is not prior to consciousness or knowledge.[23]

The last sentence comes as a shock. For it had begun to appear as if Dewey had proved the case against himself. But suddenly he reaffirms what he had maintained at the

[23] *Ibid.,* p. 6.

outset—that the infant's sensation is not prior to knowledge. But clearly there are sensations of the infant which are prior to the infant's knowledge. Dewey admits this, but avoids the obvious conclusion only by bringing in new meanings for the terms "knowledge" and "consciousness." Because he now urges that the sensation of the infant, even though it precedes the infant's knowledge, "is but an element in the world of conscious experience." This simply means, perhaps, that a pediatrician who observes the infant's behavior, will be conscious of the fact that the infant is having a sensation. The phrase "world of conscious experience" is misleading. For the objector above never intended to say that his own earliest sensations preceded everybody's knowledge, in the sense that no one could know that he was having these sensations. He only argued that his own earliest sensations preceded his own knowledge. Moreover, Dewey does not mean that the occurrence of sensations involves knowledge of some low grade and therefore that sensations are not prior to knowledge. We shall see later that he categorically denies that sensations are knowledge. Rather it is the purpose of Dewey's argument to show that the fact that we can know that infants are having sensations involves reference to a universal consciousness. He concludes as follows:

Our objector has been supposing that he could account for the origin of consciousness or knowledge because he could account for the process by which the given knowledge of a given individual came about. But if he accounts for this by something which is not known . . . he is leaving the psychological standpoint to take the ontological [à la Hume]; if he accounts for it by a known something, as a sensation produced by the reaction of a nervous organism upon a stimulus, he is accounting for its origin from something which exists for and within consciousness. Consequently he is not accounting for the origin of consciousness or knowledge as such at all. He is simply accounting for the origin of an individual consciousness, or a specific group of known facts, by reference to the larger group of known facts or *universal consciousness*.[24]

The introduction of the concept of universal consciousness is not so innocuous as it may seem. It is not merely accepted as a device for saying that my sensations may be objects of other people's knowledge or that the distinction between object and subject of knowledge arises in the course of some person's experience. Dewey gets more far-reaching results than one would expect. He argues "that the becoming of consciousness exists for consciousness only and hence that consciousness can never have become at all. That for which all origin and change exists, can never have originated or changed." [25] The arrival at this consequence is a neat sample of idealistic sleight-of-hand. From the fact that growth of consciousness in one individual may be consciously observed by others Dewey infers that there is an eternal consciousness always existing, and constantly waiting to embrace any individual consciousness as it comes into existence. This same concept of eternal consciousness was used by idealists against any account of knowledge as something which appears in the course of organic evolution. Yet indirectly it had its progressive influence too. It created a schema which later became the core of Dewey's naturalism. The most important element in the schema was the bond which supposedly existed between subject and object of knowledge. If both are viewed as elements in a larger organic whole, it becomes difficult to have dualisms of an "inner-outer" variety. For in the above argument the infant's sensation is taken as just as knowable as the object which creates the sensation. A psychologist is regarded as able to record scientifically certain facts about this relation. The relation between consciousness and its object is not one between an image in "my" mind and the object "out there." My empirical consciousness is something whose traits can be known by the psychologist. This is what is meant by saying that the sensation and the object whose impact with the infant brings the sensation about are both elements or objects of universal consciousness.

Without avowing a behaviorist approach, he thus prepares for one. He puts human behavior on a par with the behavior of nonhuman things. Granted, he does this by resorting to the dubious universal consciousness. But once the dubious aspects of this entity are dropped, Dewey has the outline of his present theory of knowledge. He need only convert the universal consciousness into nature, the individual into the organism, and the object of knowledge into environment. The result, translated into naturalistic terms, is that the organism and its environment are both parts of nature. It follows that whatever holds true of nature in general, holds true of human organisms in particular, and that the activity or capacity known as "knowledge" appears in man in accordance with the principles of organic evolution.

At this early date, however, the universal consciousness had not been naturalized; it was just what the idealists meant by it. Consequently it was distinct from the individual consciousness. In terms of this distinction, idealism set up two independent studies.[26] Philosophy was to examine the universal consciousness and psychology the individual consciousness. The distinction was very important for the idealists, because it helped philosophy in the struggle to prove its autonomy. Many idealists were trying to defend themselves against those who regarded the similarity of idealism and psychology as an indication of the worthlessness of philosophy. The anti-idealists had

---

[26] The distinction appears most clearly in the writings of E. Caird. See in particular his article "Metaphysics," *Encyclopaedia Britannica,* ninth edition.

argued: since philosophy has come to the conclusion that knowing an object means being conscious of the universal self, that is, being self-conscious, and since philosophy has assigned to itself the job of studying self-consciousness, why not merge philosophy with psychology? Self-consciousness seemed like no less a psychological concept than consciousness.

Dewey was one of those who felt that philosophy should ally itself with psychology, particularly since his study of the new psychology had left him with a higher opinion of psychology than most idealists had. He expressed himself on this point in his second paper in *Mind*. In it he repudiates flatly the distinction of Caird and the others.

No such disinction in the nature of man as that in one aspect he is "part of the partial world," and hence the subject of a purely natural science, psychology, and in another the conscious subject for which all exists, the subject of philosophy, can be maintained.[27]

In his attack on the idealists he uses their own weapons. He charges them with a dualism. He refuses to admit— granted even that a universal consciousness as distinct from an individual consciousness exists—that this universal consciousness can be known in any way apart from its manifestation in man. At this point in his development Dewey is still prepared to countenance as shady a concept as the absolute consciousness, but he construes it so as to talk about it simply by referring to its observable manifestations in man's behavior. Very soon after (in 1892), he comes to recognize that the universal self is superfluous, and what is even more important, that the individual self can be described in a thoroughly behavioristic fashion.

The most immediate consequence of the reasoning in this paper was that the philosopher must be a psychologist.

[27] *Mind*, XI (1886), 153–173.

This helps explain why Dewey's first book was his *Psychology;* it also explains Dewey's belief (expressed in the Preface) that it would serve as an introduction to philosophy.[28]

28 *Psychology,* p. v (appears in all editions).

CHAPTER FOUR

THE FIRST THREE BOOKS

Dewey's *Psychology* appeared in 1887. It was quickly followed by his *Leibniz's New Essays concerning the Human Understanding,* in 1888, and his *Applied Psychology* (written with J. A. McLellan), in 1889. The *Psychology,* as we have already noted, was an attempt to synchronize idealist epistemology and the latest developments in psychological research; the *Applied Psychology* was Dewey's first venture into the field of education; the book on Leibniz was written in the series edited by Morris and was therefore a celebration of German philosophy. The elements in Dewey's thought which we have already observed continue unabated. His attachment to Hegel, Green, and Caird becomes even more evident, and consequently his attacks on dualism, passivity, and formalism become more detailed.

Psychology is defined at the beginning of the text as the science of the facts or phenomena of self. The self has the power of recognizing itself as a separate personality. Therefore it does not merely exist, in the way sticks and stones do, but it also knows that it exists. Consequently it is said to be "conscious." [1] Each individual self is characterized by phenomena which are studied by psychology. These facts or phenomena are reported by the individual. And what he reports is something about his own self, not about anybody

---

[1] *Psychology,* pp. 1–2 (all references, unless otherwise stated, are to the first edition).

else's self. Facts of the self, therefore, must be distinguished from the facts dealt with by sciences like physics and chemistry. Dewey says: "A fact of psychology does not . . . lie open to the observation of all. It is directly and immediately known only to the self which experiences it. It is a fact of *my* or *your* consciousness, and only of mine or yours." [2] On the other hand the facts of physics and chemistry "can be known as directly and immediately by one as by another." [3]

It is when Dewey restricts himself to the individual consciousness that he can make this distinction. When the statements in the *Psychology* are compared with those we considered in our discussion of Dewey's paper "The Psychological Standpoint," there seems to be a contradiction in Dewey's position. For in that paper the infant was experiencing sensations, that is, certain psychological phenomena were taking place, which Dewey said were known, even though the infant did not know about them. If we recall the sense in which these psychological facts were said to be known, we see that what Dewey meant was that they were elements in "conscious experience," in other words, that someone, not necessarily the infant himself, knew that certain psychological phenomena were taking place. The fact that the infant was having a sensation appeared there, not in the consciousness of the infant, but in universal consciousness. But in the early pages of the *Psychology* Dewey does not avail himself of the notion of universal consciousness. Consequently the facts of the self are said to be directly and immediately known only to the self which experiences those facts.

The above does not mean that Dewey drops the notion of universal consciousness by the time he writes his *Psychology*. He introduces it gradually, by subtle devices. He gets to it by exploiting his distinction between the facts of physics and the facts of psychology. This distinction is expressed by saying that the first are universal facts and the second individual facts. Universal facts (Dewey would have said "public facts" later in his career) are constantly being discovered by scientists. In this way universal facts are transferred into the consciousness of the scientist; he becomes conscious of universal facts. Knowledge therefore, the process by which scientists become conscious of facts, is defined "as the process by which some universal element—that is, element which is in possible relation to all intelligences—is given individual form, or existence in consciousness." It follows that "Knowledge is not an individual possession. . . . To obtain knowledge, the individual must get rid of the features which are peculiar to him and conform to the conditions of universal intelligence. The realization of this process, however, must occur in an individual." The phrase "universal intelligence" is a new one to the student reading the text. This is the first mention of what Dewey called the "universal consciousness" earlier.

Thus far we have dealt only with conscious knowledge or facts. But the individual consciousness takes part in volition or acts as well. In the case of volition, too, Dewey postulates a universal "content" which embraces all possible acts before they are committed. Thus he says:

The content of every act that I can perform already exists, i. e., is universal. But it has no existence for consciousness, does not come within the range of psychology, until *I* or some *self*, perform the act, and thus give it an individual existence. It makes no difference whether the act be to write a sentence or tell the truth. In one case the pen, the ink, the paper, the hand with its muscles, and the laws of physical action which control writing already exist, and all I can do is to give these separate universal existences an *individual* existence by reproducing them in my consciousness through an act of my own. In the other case the essence of the truth already exists, and all the self can do is to make it its own. It can give it individual *form* by reproducing this universal existence in consciousness or self.[4]

The postulation of so convenient a check room, which holds bits of knowledge and acts of will until they are picked up by a particular individual, leads to another definition of psychology. Now, "psychology is the science of the reproduction of some universal content or existence, whether of knowledge or of action, in the form of individual, unsharable consciousness." [5]

Here we have the individual consciousness manifesting or reproducing the universal consciousness in the manner described one year earlier in "The Psychological Standpoint." A long passage from that paper will make evident how Dewey conceived these two kinds of consciousness. He says:

The case stands thus: We are to determine the nature of everything, subject and object, individual and universal, as it is found within conscious experience. Conscious experience testifies, in the primary aspect, my individual self is a "transition," is a process of becoming. But it testifies also that this individual self is conscious of the transition, that it knows the process by which it has become. In short, the individual self can take the universal self as its standpoint, and thence know its own origin. In so doing, it knows that it has its origin which exists for the universal self, and that therefore the universal self has never become. Consciousness testifies that consciousness is a result, but that it is the result of consciousness. Consciousness is the self-related. Stated from the positive side, consciousness has shown that it involves within itself a process of becoming, and that this process becomes conscious of itself. This process is the individual consciousness; but since it is conscious of itself, it is consciousness of the universal consciousness. All consciousness, in short, is self-consciousness, and the self is the universal consciousness, for which all process is and which, therefore, always is. The individual consciousness is but the process of realization of universal consciousness through itself. Looked at as a process, as realizing, it is individual consciousness; looked at as

4 *Ibid.*, pp. 5–6.   5 *Ibid.*, p. 6.

produced or realized, as conscious of the process, that is, of itself, it is universal consciousness.[6]

The concept of universal mind or universal consciousness is essential to Dewey's discussion of knowledge in the *Psychology*.

Knowledge, like feeling and will, is treated by considering its materials, its processes, and its results.[7] The materials for knowledge are sensations. Sensation is defined in the *Applied Psychology* as "any mental state which arises from a bodily stimulus, and upon the basis of which we get knowledge of the world around us." [8] These sensations are "presentative" or "immediate." "By *immediate* is meant that the last antecedent of the mental state is a physical change and not an intervening psychical process." [9] For instance, sensations of yellow, and of the peculiar taste and smell of an orange, follow as soon as the eye, or proper organ, is directed upon the fruit. The mind, Dewey says, does not have to remember, or imagine, or think in order to have these feelings. Knowledge, on the other hand, is not presentative or immediate; it is "mediate." This difference is illustrated by considering the difference between simply hearing a sound, and comprehending the meaning of the words uttered. "The

---

[6] *Mind,* XI, 19.

[7] There were two fundamental divisions in Dewey's early psychology. The subject as a whole was first divided into a study of knowledge, feeling, and will. Then each of these was treated on the analogy of manufacturing; knowledge, feeling, and will were each regarded as beginning with raw materials, subjecting them to certain processes, and concluding with finished products. The manner of discussing these varied. The *Psychology* was divided into three sections—knowledge, feeling, and will. Under each of these were discussed material, processes, and results, so that there were three discussions of three different manufacturing processes, so to speak. But in the *Applied Psychology* the fundamental division is material, processes, and results. Consequently, the first section treated the raw materials of knowledge, feeling, and will; the second treated the processes involved in knowledge, feeling, and will; the third did the same for the finished products. The distinction between knowledge, feeling, and will involves no adherence to "faculty psychology." Dewey is quick to emphasize the organic unity of all three (see *Psychology,* pp. 17–21).

[8] *Applied Psychology,* p. 6.   [9] *Applied Psychology,* p. 7.

sound is heard as soon as the stimulus reaches the brain; the meaning of the words is not apprehended until certain processes of interpretation . . . are brought to bear." [10] Here we have stated two key doctrines of idealistic psychology and of Dewey's theory of knowledge, which remain with him, essentially, to this day. The first is the distinction between "having" and "knowing"; the second, a corollary, is the contention that all knowledge is mediate.

Since sensations by themselves are immediately felt, if one does not connect them with other parts of one's experience, one does not acquire knowledge. And so Dewey announces: "Sensations are not knowledge." [11] Knowledge does not consist in having feelings of heat, of contact, of color, and of sound, but these feelings and sensations "lead the mind beyond their own existence." Thus a sensation suggests other sensations, not present, and

becomes a sign or symbol of them—it *represents them.* As I look at a rose, for example, all I *see,* strictly speaking, is certain shades of color. Were my knowledge to stop short with this presentative factor, it would never occur to me that a rose was before me. But these shades of color *stand for* a certain size and shape, etc. They call up other sensations not now present, but experienced in the past; they call up also associated sensations of touch, of smell, etc. And from all these factors—the most of them being now only *representative* in character—I get the idea of a rose.[12]

Since knowledge proceeds by reading signs, or determining what our sensations represent, we must try to analyze this concept of the "sign," the so-called "representative factor." The representative or *ideal* factor is the property of representing *other* sensations. "Not being supplied from the senses, the representative factor must be supplied from within the mind itself, and is thus called 'ideal.'" But this ideal quality is not given by individual minds, rather it is given by "universal mind," in Hegel's sense. The problem for the individual mind is to extract the ideal elements which already exist. Dewey says:

The statement that knowledge is the construction by the mind of a universe must not be thought to mean that knowledge is arbitrary, or the universe a product of imagination, or of the processes of individual minds. It means that mind or intelligence is necessarily universal in its nature, and that the construction of the universe of knowledge is the necessary manifestation of this universal character of intelligence. Since the mind is universal, the world exists in the same universal or real sense with it; it is a permanent objective reality, because intelligence is a permanent objectifying activity. The knowledge of the finite individual is the process by which the individual reproduces the universal mind, and hence makes real for himself the universe, which is eternally real for the complete, absolutely universal intelligence, since involved in its self-objectifying activity of knowledge.

This passage repeats the point made in "The Psychological Standpoint." There individual consciousness was said to be the realization of universal consciousness. In the *Psychology* knowledge of the finite individual is said to be the process by which the individual reproduces the universal mind. In one case the word "consciousness" is used, in the other "mind." But the doctrine remains unchanged. To get knowledge, the finite individual must thread his way through the ideal connections instituted by absolute mind; he must individualize them; he must realize the universal, ideal self.

It was just this theory of two minds—universal and individual—that Dewey rejected when he later surrendered the idealist conception of thought. But when the *Psychology* appeared he was still for all practical purposes an idealist. True, in one [13] of his papers in *Mind* he had criticized Caird, and had argued that the universal consciousness was knowable only through its manifestation in human beings.[14]

[13] "Psychology as Philosophic Method," *Mind*, XI, 153.
[14] See above, p. 47. Dewey said, in criticizing Caird: "The absolute self-

Nevertheless he maintained that an absolute mind or intelligence exists. And it was just because he thought that such an entity exists, that he regarded the world as ideal. If the universe is the objectification of absolute mind, then it is mind-like, that is, ideal. Such a conception of mind was obviously not one which conceived the mind as located in someone's head, and hence could not be accused of practicing an "inner-outer" dualism, to use Dewey's later language. But, as we have already seen, idealism did postulate, in addition to an absolute mind, an individual mind. This individual mind had as its task the reproduction of the ideal elements. Therefore, although idealism escaped one kind of dualism, it became involved in another—just as serious. Reproduction of the absolute, as used in the *Psychology*, is just the idealist dualism that Dewey attacks in the *Studies in Logical Theory*. In 1887, however, he held to a slightly modified version of this dualism; he was prepared to countenance Hegel's two minds, if not Kant's two worlds.

This same ambivalence turns up in all aspects of Dewey's early thought. Thus, although he distinguishes between sensation and knowledge, at the same time he argues that the world is thoroughly ideal. In other words, although a sensation had by an individual is to be distinguished from

consciousness must involve within itself, as organic member of its very being and activity, this manifestation and revelation. Its being must be this realisation and manifestation. Granted that this realisation and manifestation is an act not occurring in time, but eternally completed in the nature of the Absolute, and that it occurs only 'partially' and 'interruptedly' *through* (not *in*) time, in a being like man,—the fact none the less remains that philosophy, under any theory of its nature, can deal with this absolute self-consciousness only so far as it has partially and interruptedly realised itself in man. For man, as object of his philosophy, this Absolute has existence only so far as it has manifested itself in his conscious experience. To return to our questions: If the material of philosophy be the Absolute self-consciousness, and this absolute self-consciousness *is* the realisation and manifestation of itself, and as material for philosophy exists only in so far as it has realised and manifested itself in man's conscious experience, and if psychology be the science of this realisation in man, what else can philosophy in its fulness be but psychology, and psychology but philosophy?" *Ibid.*, pp. 164–165.

knowledge, still, taken as an element which is part of the ideal universe, this sensation must have meaning or connection. This is a direct consequence of holding on to two kinds of mind. In the absolute mind every sensation leads to knowledge, and therefore every sensation has knowledge associated with it. But in the mind of individual man, some sensations lead to knowledge, others do not, simply because man can never completely realize the absolute mind.

There is still another quality of Dewey's early thought which flows from his "two minds." It appears in his discussion of the method of psychology.[15] Since the ultimate facts of psychology are all described in statements like "I feel dizzy," etc., the best way to get at them is by introspection. But introspection has its defects and difficulties, Dewey says in the section "Difficulties of Introspection." [16] Therefore it must be supplemented by the experimental, genetic, and what Dewey calls "objective" methods. The last is the most interesting from our point of view, since it involves Dewey's theory of objective mind. Objective method is "the study of the objective manifestations of mind." [17] Mind here is absolute mind. Dewey says at this point:

Mind has not remained a passive spectator of the universe, but has produced and is producing certain results. These results are objective, can be studied as all objective historical facts may be, and are permanent. They are the most fixed, certain, and universal signs to us of the way in which the mind works. Such objective manifestations of mind are, in the realm of intelligence, phenomena like language and science; in that of will, social and political institutions; in that of feeling, art; in that of the whole self, religion. Philology, the logic of science, history, sociology, etc., study these various departments as objective, and endeavor to trace the relations which connect their phenomena.[18]

The most important point is that

[15] See *Psychology*, ch. i, sec. 2; also *Applied Psychology*, p. 2.
[16] *Psychology*, ch. i, sec. 2. [17] *Ibid.*, p. 11. [18] *Ibid.*, pp. 11–12.

none of these sciences takes into account the fact that science, religion, art, etc., are all of them products of the mind or self, working itself out according to its own laws, and that, therefore, in studying them we are only studying the fundamental nature of the conscious self. It is in these wide departments of human knowledge, activity, and creation that we find most clearly revealed the laws of its activities.[19]

Objective method takes as its subject matter the universal mind. By embracing this method (*Geisteswissenschaft* or social psychology) the psychologist certainly extends his task, and Dewey does not touch on these matters in the rest of the book. But the insistence upon working with the social sciences is clear. It will be recalled [20] that this was one of the virtues of the "new psychology" for Dewey. Here, in the *Psychology*, we find the Hegelian origin of Dewey's emphasis upon the social, the conception of the individual as manifesting a larger organism which is constituted by an absolute mind. The resultant advice for the psychologist who wishes to understand the human mind is to go out and watch its results in a cultural setting. We have in the passage quoted above tracked down one of the Hegelisms to which Dewey refers when he says that he was strongly influenced by "Hegel's idea of cultural institutions as an 'objective mind.' " [21] Dewey tells us that "the metaphysical idea that an absolute mind is manifested in social institutions dropped out," and "the idea, upon an empirical basis, of the power exercised by cultural environment in shaping the ideas, beliefs, and intellectual attitudes of individuals remained." [22]

Although this Hegelian conception of objective mind served as an impetus to developing a social psychology, the very book in which the glimmerings of that future social psychology appear, is one in which the introspective method is upheld as central. This fact, I think, is also explained by

19 *Ibid.*, p. 12.
21 Schilpp, p. 17.
20 See chap. iii above.
22 *Ibid.*, p. 17.

the doctrine of two minds. This is confirmed by the following warning which Dewey appends to his discussion of the
objective method.

It must be borne in mind [he says] that in studying psychological facts by any or all of these methods [experimental, genetic,
and objective], the ultimate appeal is to self-consciousness.
None of these facts mean anything until they are thus interpreted. As objective facts they are not material of psychology,
they are still universal, and must be interpreted into *individual*
terms. . . . The psychical phenomena of infancy or the insane
would teach us nothing, because they would be nothing to us,
if we did not have the power of putting ourselves into these
states of imagination, and thus seeing what they are like.[23]

The point here should be clear. Dewey is merely repeating
idealist doctrine. He accepts its implications for social psychology, but also accepts those which lead to a conception
of social sciences as radically different from the other sciences. What Hegel gives with one hand he almost takes
away with the other. Dewey is left with a social orientation,
but also with two vague concepts—an individual ego and a
universal mind.

The papers in *Mind* and the *Psychology* were the fruits of
Dewey's first contact with English idealism. This reën-
forced, as he tells us, the idealism he got from Morris. His
book on Leibniz represents a return to Morris' way of saying
things; it is the last large work which clearly shows Morris'
hand throughout.

Morris, we saw earlier, began a series of books devoted to
demonstrating the superiority of German philosophy. His
own *Kant's Critique of Pure Reason,* one of the first in the
series, appeared in 1882. In the introduction he divided the
epochal works in the history of philosophy into three classes.
The first contained those that were "constructive." The second contained those that were "destructive," the works end-
ing "mainly in negations." The final group comprised "crit-

[23] *Psychology,* p. 12.

ical" works, works that mark transitions in the history of philosophy. According to Morris, the contributions of Plato, Aristotle, Leibniz, and Hegel were in the first class, Hume's treatise in the second, and Kant's first critique in the third.

Putting Leibniz in the same class with Hegel and Aristotle was a great compliment on Morris' part. It is not surprising, then, that a book in his series was devoted to Leibniz. It was *Leibniz's New Essays concerning the Human Understanding* by Dewey.[24] In it the author swiftly announces his allegiance to the idealist cause. He says in the Preface: "I have . . . endeavored to keep in mind, throughout, Leibniz's relations to Locke, and to show the 'Nouveaux Essais' as typical of the distinction between British and German thought." [25]

Dewey, it is to be noted, was not as violent as Morris in his antipathy to British empiricism. For Morris it was darkness on the one side and light on the other. But Dewey had already written a paper [26] in which he had argued that English philosophy before Green had something in common with the later idealist, "Germanizing" movement, as it was called by some. Consequently he could not come out as strongly as Morris had; he could not separate them completely. His deviations, however, were not great, and he could be depended upon. For this reason he could be assigned a crucial task, from Morris' crusading point of view. His book necessarily involved a discussion of the Locke-Leibniz differences, which, for Morris, marked an important point in the war against empiricism.

Because of its more general character, Dewey's work on Leibniz is an even better index of his position at that time than his *Psychology*. It points up very clearly his organic view of the world, his emphasis on activity and continuity, and his attack on dualism and formalism. Leibniz's philos-

---

[24] Hereafter referred to as "LNE."   [25] LNE, p. vii.
[26] "The Psychological Standpoint."

ophy represented, Dewey said, "the dawning consciousness of the modern world"; [27] Leibniz was the first to see that the world is a unity, that continuity prevails throughout, and that everything within it is interdependent.[28] For Leibniz the universe is an organism.[29]

This organismic conception of the universe was derived partially, Dewey says, from the new science of biology of Leibniz's time.[30] "Swammerdam, Malpighi, Leewenhoek—these are names which occur and recur in the pages of Leibniz. Indeed, he appears to be the first of that now long line of modern philosophers to be profoundly influenced by the conception of life and the categories of organic growth." [31] But even though he believed that the ideas of organism and of life are central to Leibniz's thought, Dewey did not think that reading these biologists was what directed Leibniz to his organicism. "Rather, he had already learned to think of the world as organic through and through, and found in the results of biology confirmations, apt illustrations of a truth of which he was already thoroughly convinced." [32] In a sense, this remark describes Dewey's own philosophical development. His own conception of the world as organic starts with his idealist writing and thinking. Later it is supplemented and fortified (and transformed, of course) by his contact with Darwinism. But it is very interesting to find Dewey at this early date conscious of such a process in thought patterns. The fact that he was aware of a tendency in some philosophers to begin with vaguely formulated metaphysical notions and then to sharpen them by using the results of science, facilitated his own transition to instrumentalism. Granted that Leibniz saw in biology a confirmation of his metaphysic and stopped there, whereas Dewey later went further and changed his whole philosophy to suit the results

27 LNE, p. 21.   28 Ibid., p. 22.   29 LNE, p. 62.
30 Ibid., p. 30.   31 Ibid., p. 33.   32 Ibid., p. 34.

of empirical science. Nevertheless, Dewey went through a period when he, too, saw the results of biology and psychology as "apt illustrations" and nothing more. What is distinctive of Dewey's development is that because of careful attention to results in biology and sociology and psychology, he saw that they were only superficial confirmations of idealism and that a recognition of their true significance would lead to the abandonment of idealist organicism.

The concept of organism was the major weapon Leibniz used in his attack on dualism. Leibniz, Dewey stresses, was originally a Cartesian, and Descartes a dualist. When Leibniz surrendered his Cartesianism, he appealed neither to occasionalism nor to Spinoza. He escaped both these alternatives by creating his theory of the monad, according to Dewey. Therefore Dewey pits Leibniz against Locke. For Locke, he says, took the Cartesian dualism for granted, while Leibniz recognized that "reality is an organic whole—not two parts with a chasm between them." [33]

In addition to defending Leibniz's attack on Locke's dualism, Dewey extols his criticism of Locke's theory of mind as passive. Leibniz's activism is stressed throughout the book, and his statement *Substance c'est l'action* is taken by Dewey to be "the keynote and the battle-cry of the Leibnizian philosophy." [34]

After having idolized Leibniz, throughout most of the book, Dewey spends his final chapter formulating a "criticism and conclusion." In it Leibniz is assigned with debits as well as credits. So much debit in fact, that Dewey feels constrained to conclude the chapter with the following remarks:

It would be a grievous blunder to suppose that this final chapter annihilates the earlier ones; that the failure as to method, though a failure in a fundamental point, cancelled his fundamental achievements. Such thought as that substance is activity; that its process is measured by its end, its idea; that the universe is an interrelated unit; the thoughts of organism, of continuity, of uniformity of law—introduced and treated as Leibniz treated them—are imperishable.[35]

What was this "failure as to method," so fundamental in Leibniz' work? Dewey is very explicit on this point. He says:

The fundamental contradiction in Leibniz is to be found, I believe, between the method which he adopted—without inquiry into its validity and scope—and the subject-matter, or perhaps better the attitude, to which he attempted to apply this method; between, that is to say, the scholastic formal logic on the one hand and the idea of interrelation derived from the development of scientific thought, on the other.

The Hegelian bias is clear. Leibniz thought too highly of formal logic. "The result," therefore, "is constant conflict between the method and content of his philosophy, between its letter and its spirit." [36] The conflict is twofold. First of all, "the unity of the content of his philosophy, the conception of organism or harmony is a unity which essentially involves a difference," whereas "the unity of his method is a formal identity which excludes it." [37] The language is Hegel's; the fundamental distinction is between an organic relation and a formal or mechanical relation, between organic oneness and formal oneness. Secondly, the unity of Leibniz is a "unity of activity," a "dynamic process," whereas "the unity of formal logic is exclusive of any mediation or process, and is essentially rigid and lifeless." [38]

We are left with a fairly clear picture of the implications of general philosophy for Dewey's logical views. Just as Morris' theory of mind pitted itself against British empiricism, so Dewey's theory of logic clashed with formal logic. We are now in a better position to understand some of Dewey's specifically logical writings.

---

35 *Ibid.*, p. 272.
37 *Ibid.*, p. 241.
36 LNE, p. 241.
38 *Ibid.*, p. 242.

CHAPTER FIVE

THE LOGIC OF EMPIRICISM

We have been long in coming to Dewey's theory of logic. But his critique of Leibniz prevents us from waiting any longer. We have seen his distrust of formal logic constantly growing; this appears in the article on the new psychology and throughout the papers in *Mind,* as well as in the last chapter of the book on Leibniz. The Hegelian doctrine is clearly responsible for the general outline of Dewey's thought on this point. He opposes formal logic, but what substitute does he have? Hegel's was one, of course. But then there were more recent logics, those produced by British idealists. Although neither Green [1] nor Edward Caird had written a book on logic, in 1883 Bradley's *Principles of Logic* was published, Lotze's *Logic* appeared in English in 1884, and in 1888 Bosanquet, the translator of Lotze, presented his own *Logic.*

The general attitude among idealists at the time was that Bradley's work came opportunely.[2] They had had too much of formal logic, and were sorely in need of a comprehensive formulation of their objections and of their positive views on the nature of thought. What they wanted was an account of the methods of thinking which would steer clear of the neo-Kantian formalism of Hamilton as well as avoid the errors of British empiricism. Mill represented the latter,

---

1 There were, of course, Green's *Lectures* on logic, which will be discussed later.

2 See Robert Adamson's critical notice of Bradley's book in *Mind,* 1884, pp. 122 ff.

and even though he was no formalist, from the idealist point of view he presented just as many difficulties.

In the light of this double opposition to Hamilton and Mill on the part of the idealists, it is not surprising to find Dewey in their camp. For he had been treated to similar opinions in the writings of Morris. It will be recalled that Hamilton and Mill by no means exhausted all positions for Morris, and that Dewey in his earliest papers rejected the psychology of empiricism in its British, Kantian, and neo-Kantian forms. And since the chief problem of logic for the idealists was the analysis of actual thought, it is not surprising that the first logical writings of Dewey appear in his *Psychology,* in the chapter entitled "Thinking." [8]

In this chapter thinking is defined "as knowledge of universal elements; that is, of ideas as such, or of relations." [4] Thinking seizes upon the ideal element in facts, and therefore its objects are generals or properties. You cannot think about a particular object unless you first clothe it conceptually, so to speak. Therefore the first item discussed in the chapter on thinking is the concept. [5]

The section on the concept in the third revised edition (1891) is very important. In it we find rumblings of Dewey's later view of ideas as "plans of action." Its central distinc-

---

[8] The list of readings at the end of this chapter gives one a good picture of the books on thinking Dewey was reading at that time. They may be divided into two groups. First, a whole series of books on metaphysics and psychology, with particular reference to passages on conception, abstraction, judgment, and reasoning. Some of them are: Hamilton's *Lectures on Metaphysics,* Porter's *The Human Intellect,* Lewes' *Problems of Life and Mind,* Murray's *Handbook of Psycholoby,* Sully's *Outlines of Psychology,* Bain's *The Senses and the Intellect,* Taine's *De l'intelligence,* and Spencer's *Principles of Psychology.* The second group consists mainly of Bradley's *Principles of Logic* and the nineteenth-century German logic-books of Lotze, Sigwart, Wundt, and Bergman. Bosanquet's *Logic* had not yet appeared.

[4] *Psychology,* p. 202.

[5] The concept is followed by the judgment and then by reasoning. This tripartite analysis of reasoning had long been common. Dewey calls them the three "aspects" of thinking, the word "aspect" being used lest hard-and-fast faculties for each be postulated.

tion is between an immediately felt state and the function of that state.[6] Failure to distinguish between an entity and its function is held responsible for all the meaningless discussion of the nature of concepts. "It is as if," Dewey says, "in physiology writers were to discuss the heart without having first decided whether they were writing of the *thing*, or of the *work* done by that thing."[7] The distinction is to be carried out in the case of concepts. First there is an image associated with the concept. This image, however, is particular; it is not the concept. It is a mental state, and as such a "bare existence." "The nominalist," Dewey says, "is therefore, quite right when he asserts that there is no such thing as a general idea—provided he is speaking of mental existences. . . . But so speaking, he does not touch the question at all."[8] A concept, according to Dewey, is not a mental existence, but "the *power* which a particular image has of standing for or conveying a certain meaning or intellectual value . . . the concept is something which the image does; some meaning which it conveys."[9]

The image is identified with the percept, and so the relation between image and concept is that between percept and concept. And since the concept is what the image conveys, "the concept arises from the percept *through realizing the full meaning im*-plied but not *ex*-plicit in the percept." Despite the fact that the concept arises from the percept, Dewey says that knowledge of any particular percept gives

[6] This point is discussed at greatest length in Dewey's article "How Do Concepts Arise from Percepts," *Public School Journal*, XI (November, 1891), 128–130. Substantially the same position is taken in the third revised edition of the *Psychology*.

[7] "How Do Concepts Arise from Percepts," *Public School Journal* (XI), 128. If such an ambiguity were permitted, Dewey says, "it would not be surprising if one school of physiologists held the heart to be a definite, isolated thing, of a certain shape and size composed of certain fibers, while another school held the heart to be a factor or member in an interconnected unity; not a thing but an activity: and its special structure a matter of indifference compared with the general purpose subserved by this structure."

[8] *Ibid.*, p. 128.   [9] *Ibid.*, p. 128.

no *general* knowledge. Speaking of a particular percept, for example, that of a triangle, he says:

Knowledge of it from this point of view would be exhausted in getting its exact shape, size, length of sides, degree of angles, stuff made of, color, etc. The mind would nowhere be led beyond the consideration of the bare thing present. Even if it were found that the sum of its three interior angles was equal to two right angles, this would be a trait of the particular triangle, a bare item of information of no more general value than that the length of one side was $1\frac{2}{17}$ inches.

Dewey then adds:

Suppose the mind advances beyond the particular triangle to the thought that there is a principle involved in the triangle; that the triangle, like everything in the world, is made upon a certain principle which is embodied in it; that this principle furnishes the plans and specifications according to which anything must exist in order to be a triangle at all. What shall we call this principle? Is it not evident that since it is this principle which constitutes the particular thing a triangle, rather than a pumpkin or a stove-pipe, it is this principle we really mean by triangle, and are attempting to know? Well, it is this principle which forms the concept "triangle." The concept "triangle," in other words, is the way in which three lines are put together; it is a mode or form of construction.[10]

It is not difficult to discern that Dewey is here subscribing to the familiar constructivist theory of mathematical definitions. The essence of the theory is the belief that a definition which involves in its *definiens* a statement telling how to construct the object in question is more desirable than one which does not. Thus Dewey, in the passage cited, believes that the proper definition of a triangle is one which calls it the kind of polygon which involves putting three line-segments together in a certain way. He rejects as inadequate a definition which calls a triangle a polygon the sum of whose interior angles is equal to two right angles. His argument for this choice is not very clear. At one point

10 *Ibid.*, pp. 128–129.

he criticizes the nonconstructive definition for failing to achieve generality. But this is obviously false. The nonconstructive definition is just as general as the other; it presents a necessary and sufficient condition for being a triangle, which is exactly what the constructive definition does. When Dewey says that even if it were found that the particular polygon under consideration in the above-cited passage had the property of its interior angles, adding up to two right angles, that this would be a bare item of information of no more general value than that the length of one side was $1\frac{2}{17}$ inches, he is wrong. We know that the trait concerning the sum of the angles is characteristic of all triangles, whereas having one side's length be $1\frac{2}{17}$ inches is not. One may criticize him in another way. One may say that if having its interior angles add up to 180 degrees is a fact no more general than having one side $1\frac{2}{17}$ inches long, then the property of being constructed in a certain way possesses just as little generality. In short, the choice of the constructive definition cannot be based on considerations of generality.

It would not be worth while to press this criticism at this point. Leaving the evaluation of Dewey's argument for a moment, we should point out that the defense of constructive definitions prepares the way for a very general epistemological judgment on Dewey's part. For he says, after arguing as he did above, that "the only way to know the triangle is to make it—to go through the act of putting together the lines in the way called for." [11]

The emphasis upon construction and genesis is crucial in this article. Dewey took the constructivist theory of mathematical concepts, a theory with a long and varied history, and worked it into a genetic or evolutionary approach. The constructive definition is preferred because it presents the origin of the thing. To know a thing com-

[11] *Ibid.*, p. 129.

pletely, he argues, is to know it in "its mode of genesis . . .
in its relations and bearings." You must know "how it came
to be so." [12] This constructivism is tied up with his Hegelian
desire to emphasize change, the Darwinian emphasis upon
origin, and an interest in educational theory. This last is
of great interest because the article from which we have
quoted appeared in an educational journal, and because
its chief conclusion was that the analysis "reveals the impossibility of external or mechanical or external instruction." "If a concept is the true meaning of a thing, and this
true meaning is a mode of mental action, a process of intellectual construction, how possibly can true information
be externally conveyed from one to another?" The answer
is that it cannot. Thus we see why the motto of Dewey's
Applied Psychology was "Learn to Do by Knowing and to
Know by Doing."

Constructivism is not pragmatism, and we cannot take
these early writings as anything but the very beginnings
of Dewey's doctrine as we know it today. At this point many
of the most significant of Dewey's views have not yet appeared. For instance, the formulation of the theory of the
concept still has mentalistic hangovers. Although the illustration suggests the importance of overt activity, Dewey
still talks about the concept as a mode of mental action.
And so despite all the avowals of opposition to dualism, he
still gives a suggestion that the action or construction is in
some way going on only in the recesses of some geometer's
head. Nevertheless, this is an important beginning; it is
one of Dewey's earliest observations with a pragmatist ring.

At about the same time that he was emphasizing the constructive aspect of the concept, Dewey was beginning to
write explicitly on logic. In 1890 his first lengthy piece with
the word "logic" in its title appeared—"Is Logic a Dualistic
Science?" This was a review and criticism of Venn's *Prin-*

12 *Ibid.,* p. 129.

ciples of Empirical or Inductive Logic. It appeared in the
Open Court just one year before Dewey's *Outlines of a
Critical Theory of Ethics* appeared and also a year before
the article on concepts and percepts.[13]

Dewey regarded Venn's book as a contribution to the
movement he called "The Newer Logic." This movement,
he said, was engaged in "an attempt to take account of the
methods of thinking employed by science, that is, of the
methods the aim of which is truth, and which deal with a
material of fact." [14] He contrasts it with the formalist movement, calling the latter "an attempt to deal with thinking
in vacuo, that is with methods which leave out (or abstract
from) the material of fact, and which have no aim except non-contradiction of their own premises—self-consist-
ency." [15] And so the logicians are divided into two camps
—those who are interested in the logic of argument, not
of truth, and those whose concern is the logic of science,
the empirical study of actual knowledge. Among those
mentioned as students of the newer logic are Lotze, Sigwart, Wundt, Jevons, Bradley, and Bosanquet. Then Venn
is added, only with the qualification that his work is "written from a philosophical standpoint differing from that of
most of the foregoing names." But Venn's book did have,
according to Dewey, an aim in common with those of the
other logicians—even the idealist ones—because it treated
"thinking as a process having relation to truth."

The tendency to classify logicians in this way was common among English idealists. For instance, T. H. Green

13 In 1890 Dewey also published a series of short book reviews which
permit us to observe his general philosophical position at the time. In the
Andover Review he reviewed E. Caird, *The Critical Philosophy of Immanuel Kant;* Mahaffy and Bernard, *Kant's Critical Philosophy for English
Readers;* and Sterret, *Studies in Hegel's Philosophy of Religion.* These
reviews indicate opposition to dualism and continued adherence to Hegel,
also intense opposition to British empiricism and formal logic.

14 *Open Court,* III, 2040.   15 *Ibid.,* p. 2040.

begins his lectures on *The Logic of the Formal Logicians* [16] with the following statement: "As to the office of logic, there are two principal views among modern writers, (*a*) that of the 'formal logicians,' of whom Hamilton and Mansel are specimens, (*b*) that of all others, the view that logic is the science of the method of knowledge." [17] Into this latter group of nonformal logicians Green puts Mill, Kuno Fischer, Sigwart, and Ueberweg. And just as Dewey distinguished Venn from the other methodologists, so Green divided the nonformal logicians into two subgroups. He says that although these nonformal logicians agree that logic is the science of the method of knowledge, "their views of *what* the method of knowledge is vary according to the difference in their notions of what the object of knowledge is." [18] These lectures on the formal logicians were delivered by Green as the first part of his *Lectures on Logic,* the second part treating *The Logic of J. S. Mill.* Nettleship, Green's editor, tells us that both parts take the form, "not of a systematic exposition of the subject, but of a commentary and criticism on H. L. Mansel and J. S. Mill, the most representative of the writers on logic who were at that time studied in Oxford." [19]

Green's failure to develop a systematic logic was felt keenly. It was not until the publication of Bradley's *Prin-*

[16] *Works of Thomas Hill Green*, II, 158–194.
[17] *Ibid.*, p. 158.   [18] *Ibid.*, p. 158.
[19] *Ibid.*, p. 157n. It should be observed here that depending upon which basis for classification was employed, Mill and Hamilton were in one case grouped together, and in another separated. As British empiricists in their theory of knowledge, Morris and Dewey linked them and thereby separated them both from the idealists. But as a formal logician Hamilton was separated from Mill, the later being grouped with idealist methodologists, in so far as he was a methodologist. This explains any apparent inconsistency in the position Dewey took on Hamilton and Mill. Later, moreover, it will be observed how the grounds for putting Mill and the idealists in the same class are called into question by Dewey. For later Mill and the empirical logicians generally are also accused of holding to a "formalist" conception of thought, despite their avowals to the contrary.

ciples, as we have seen, that a detailed exposition of idealist methodology was available in English. For this reason, Robert Adamson, in his view of Bradley's book, said:

It is not many years since one might have said that, on the whole, putting aside the merely historical teaching of what is erroneously entitled the Aristotelian logic, English writing on the subject might have been fairly distributed under two main heads: on the one hand, a purely formal logic, basing itself, though perhaps unwittingly, on an extremely imperfect psychology, supporting itself by appeal to the high authority of Kant, and claiming to have effected, if at a cost of rejecting the most interesting questions, a purification and scientific limitation of the sphere of logical discussions; on the other hand, a general theory of knowledge, likewise involving much disputable psychology, but rightly claiming to represent more truthfully than its rival the actual process of thought as exemplified in scientific work, and so extending its boundaries as to be able only by arbitrary refusal to reject the deeper questions inevitably raised by any discussion of the nature of knowledge.[20]

The two groups Adamson refers to are composed exclusively of English logicians. He is, of course, distinguishing between the Mansel-Hamilton group and the English inductive logicians, led by Mill.

The net result of this feverish drawing of lines and making of alliances was to show that the worst thing one could do was to be a formal logician, the next worse thing one could be was an inductive logician, and the thing one had to be was an idealist logician. There was, therefore, in addition to a theory of good logic, also a theory of the lesser evil. Mill, for instance, was not as bad as Mansel, simply because Mill was supposed to have studied actual thought, actual scientific activity. Therefore for an idealist Mill was the lesser evil. But an idealist could admit only so much in Mill's favor. Because viewed in the light of the truths of idealism Mill had a defective psychology which could not

[20] This review appears as the fourth of a series of supplementary articles in Adamson, *A Short History of Logic.*

be overlooked and which in certain respects was just as bad as Mansel's and Hamilton's. Morris had made a related point when he called Hamilton an intuitional empiricist and Mill an empirical empiricist.[21] Therefore the British idealists and Morris combined to furnish Dewey with the foundations for his consideration of Venn. Venn was a descendant of Mill (Venn avows this in the Preface to his *Principles of Empirical or Inductive Logic*), and so he inherits many of Mill's infirmities. The most important, the one Mill got from his father, and his father, ultimately, from Locke, was dualism. The specter appears once more.

The question Dewey asks—"Is Logic a Dualistic Science?"—is motivated by the following very direct statements by Venn in his Preface.

Our first postulate . . . is simply the resolution to start with a *duality* of existences, our sensations and ideas on the one hand, and the material of a world of phenomena on the other.[22]

What we have to take for granted in Logic is, then, a duality, external and internal. On the one hand, outside us, there is the world of phenomena pursuing its course; and, on the other hand, within us, there is the observing and thinking mind. Logic is concerned with the judgments of the latter about the former.[23]

According to Venn's view there are some sciences, like psychology, which deal only with mental processes, and others, like physics, which deal with "external phenomena." But logic is held to be different from both of these in so far as it "has to do with the processes of the human mind when judging about phenomena." Venn seems to hold to the conventional empiricist distinction between an inner and an outer world. Accordingly Dewey maintains that on Venn's view, "the sun is there," "my idea of the sun is here."

[21] "Philosophy and Its Specific Problems," *Princeton Review*, IX (1882), 215.
[22] *Principles of Empirical or Inductive Logic*, pp. 3-4.
[23] *Ibid.*, pp. 21-22.

Therefore, Dewey argues, Venn's logic must begin with a dualism and then go on to consider how the idea may be brought into conformity with the object. This raises the following question: "Are there, for logic at least, two worlds, of which one has to be brought into conformity with the other, or is there but one world, and that one logical through and through?" [24] Dewey's answer, a little further on, is direct: "There is but one world, the world of knowledge, not two, an inner and an outer, a world of observation and a world of conception; and this one world is everywhere logical." [25]

But Venn, Dewey points out, did not maintain in all passages that objects are simply "given," that there is a world of objects totally unrelated to mind. Venn had said, for instance, "we postulate a world or aggregate of objects —not out of relation to human faculties in general, which would be absurd—but conditioned in relation to our representative state of faculties." [26] Venn had also denied that the "problem of knowledge" required an answer to the question "in what sense [do] our ideas 'resemble' or are [they] 'copies of' actual external objects." [27] The elements in the "duality" which Venn thought it was necessary to postulate were conception on the one hand, and perception on the other. The crucial question for Dewey, therefore, is:

How are perception and observation logically related to thinking, to conception? Does logic take up its task when these are furnished to it, ready-made, thus having a dualistic basis, or do logical processes enter equally into both perception and conception, so that from a certain standpoint, each has a logical character? [28]

Dewey may be more easily understood if one realizes what he meant by "perception." Perception is not sensation; this is very important. Sensation is a mere having, but percep-

---

[24] *Open Court*, III, 2041.   [25] *Ibid.*, p. 2043.
[26] *Op. cit.*, p. 16.   [27] *Op. cit.*, p. 28.   [28] *Open Court*, III, 2041.

tion is a stage of knowledge. True, it is "the original and least developed, that is, most particular, form of knowledge." [29] Nevertheless, it *is* knowledge; the results of a perception may be formulated in a judgment. Moreover, perception is the germ of all other knowledge. "The other stages of knowledge *are developed from perception* by a natural process of growth." [30] Therefore it is surely not cut off from conception or abstract scientific thought, even though it is a less developed and more particular form of knowledge. The view against which Dewey was fighting, which he thought Venn defended, was the

theory in psychology that individual objects are impressed upon the mind as wholes without any constructive activity of the mind. . . . The activity of the mind from this point on was supposed to consist in combining and separating these wholes, so that the results are more or less artificial in nature, and constitute a departure from the simple realities made known to us in perception. But this theory falls into a double error. In the first place, perception or knowledge of particular things is not a passive operation of impressions, but involves the active integration of various experiences. It is a process of reaching out after the fullest and richest experience possible. In illustration, consider the process of scientific observation. The mind does not wait for sensations to be forced upon it, but goes out in search of them. . . . Secondly, such processes as imagination and thinking are not mechanically working *upon* percepts, but are their transformation and enrichment in accordance with the same law of a demand for the unified maximum of meaning. Thinking transforms perception by bringing out elements latent in it.[31]

Perception and conception are simply two different stages of knowledge. It follows that perception involves thought and inference and that the object perceived is not the result of mere impact upon the perceiver. In this way we get the beginnings of Dewey's theory that the object of thought is

---

[29] *Psychology*, p. 158; also see *Applied Psychology*, p. 91.
[30] *Applied Psychology*, p. 93.   [31] *Psychology*, pp. 157–158.

constructed by thought. Venn had argued that empirical logic began by assuming the existence of ready-made objects. He admitted, as we saw earlier, that these objects were constructed, but said that he was not concerned with the history of their construction. He had said:

Select whatever object we please,—the most apparently simple in itself, and the most definitely parted off from others that we can discover,—yet we shall find ourselves constrained to admit that a considerable mental process had been passed through before that object could be recognized as being an object, that is as possessing some degree of unity and as requiring to be distinguished from other unities.[32]

Although Venn insists that analysis and synthesis take place in forming the idea of an object, he also insists that they occur before logic takes up its task. Dewey, opposing Venn on the latter point, argues that the logician must study and report on these processes. Venn believed that the logician only had "to insist that extensive results of such a process must be presupposed at every assigned time and place at which the thinker may be supposed to appeal to his logic." But Venn did not think he had to do anything more than insist upon this fact, "unless he proposes to set to work to discuss the rational development of the human race from its first commencement: in other words to make his logic a chapter in evolutionary Psychology." [33]

Dewey was not deterred by the charge that what he really wanted to study was evolutionary psychology. He was convinced that the material Venn wished to relegate to psychology was a proper concern of empirical logic, and he refused to separate the study of our knowledge of objects from the study of other processes of the mind. He felt that they were no less "logical" than the processes Venn studied. Dewey's strongest argument rests upon the concessions of Venn we quoted above. Dewey says:

---

[32] *Op. cit.*, pp. 5–6.   [33] *Op. cit.*, p. 9.

Mr. Venn shows clearly and decisively, to my mind, that in the most elementary recognition of an object processes of analysis and synthesis of very considerable complexity are involved.[34]

Dewey continues:

As soon as we give up the view that objects are presented to the mind already distinguished from others and united in cohering wholes, we are tacitly admitting that logical processes enter into the recognition or observation of facts. When we go further and say that the individual object becomes such to us only through a process of mental synthesis and analysis, it seems to me that the admission is more than tacit—it is express. The only ground on which the logical character of recognition could be denied, would be that mental analysis and synthesis are not logical processes. I hardly think Mr. Venn would take this position; still less can I see how he or anyone else would uphold it.[35]

The main point of this attack on Venn was Dewey's belief that all propositions, even those established on the basis of perception, are arrived at inferentially. It follows that if the logician is to study inference then he must study the manner in which these perceptual propositions are arrived at, as well as that in which the most general propositions of science are established. All these propositions are regarded as hypotheses. Thus he says, "Our first perceptions of objects, being due to analysis and synthesis, are in a sense, tentative hypotheses which we form in order to account for our experiences." [36] He remarks, however, that from the standpoint of common language, it sounds absurd to say that the statement "the fire burns" is a hypothesis.

[34] At this point Dewey refers to an illustration in Venn's book, which, interestingly enough, he again uses in the first edition of *How We Think*. Venn had said, to use Dewey's paraphrasing of his point, that "to expect a dog who could not exercise quite a complex analysis and synthesis to perceive a rainbow, would be hardly more reasonable than to expect him to 'see' the progress of democracy in the place where he lives—although the ultimate constituent sensible events are as accessible to his observation as they are to ours." See *Principles of Empirical or Inductive Logic*, pp. 7, 143–144.

[35] *Open Court*, III, 2042.   [36] *Ibid.*, p. 2042.

But from the logical standpoint, it is far from being absurd. Whence the whole chemical theory of combustion, and what is the need of it?—unless the first judgment that "the fire burns" is, after all, only a tentative and crude analytic-synthetic process, needing to be carried farther to be corrected, and, finally, transformed into a hypothesis more nearly agreeing with the facts. If this is not evident, substitute the judgment "the sun moves" for the one "the fire burns."

Dewey concludes that

. . . ordinary perception and scientific reflection have just the same material, and follow, in rough, the same methods. There is hypothesis, induction, inference, classification, analysis, synthesis, whatever logical processes you please to take in the perception of the sun as shining. . . . Even our estimate of paleness,—a color pure and simple,—psychological analysis shows to be no ultimate datum, but in great part an inference.[37]

From a historical point of view the review of Venn is significant in so far as it shows that Dewey's belief in the continuity of ordinary perception and scientific conception began from idealist premises. It began with the contention that all knowledge is the development of that which was implicit in perception. All the "stages of knowledge" that Dewey so laboriously discussed in the *Psychology* are stages in the progressive unfolding of the content of perception. He therefore presents perception as continuous with the most remote and abstract theories in physics and thus prevents any of the dualistic splits between perception and conception. This unity of perception and conception is the idealist forerunner of the slogan of instrumentalism—"the unity of theory and practice."

[37] *Ibid.*, p. 2043.

CHAPTER SIX

THE LOGIC OF VERIFICATION

In the same year, 1890, Dewey wrote an extended consideration of the position he had suggested in the review of Venn's
book. It also appeared in the *Open Court,* and was called
"The Logic of Verification." In it he was troubled by one
possible objection to his position. He says,

> To this doctrine an objection after this fashion might be
> raised: Such a conception makes the process of verification
> impossible. If there is but one realm of knowledge, what is the
> standard of truth? With what shall we compare our *ideas* in
> order to verify them? If logic has a dualistic basis, the question
> is easily answered; on the one hand there is the world of con-
> ceptions, on the other the world of perceptions, of facts. And
> we test our ideas by comparing them with facts. But upon the
> theory of a single realm of knowledge, logical throughout, no
> such comparison and testing is possible. It seems upon this
> theory that the only criterion of truth is the consistency of
> ideas with themselves, and everyone knows that ideas may be
> self-consistent, and yet untrue, or even highly absurd.[1]

Dewey's reconsideration of his point of view is dictated by
a sensitivity to the difficulties of a coherence theory of truth.
And in a sense the "Logic of Verification" is an attempt to
steer between the coherence theory on the one side and
a correspondence theory on the other. The discussion is not
very clear, chiefly because of the constant use of two vague
terms—"idea" and "fact." Nevertheless it contains many
terms—"idea" and "fact." Nevertheless it is important because it marks a departure from idealistic logic.

[1] *Open Court,* IV, 2226.

Dewey first attacks the correspondence theory of truth in an interesting way. If we are to test our ideas by their correspondence with the world, he says, then we assume that "this real world, the actual facts, are known." But if they are known, why do we go to the trouble to form a hypothesis about them? he asks.

If we already know the facts, it certainly seems a waste of energy and of time to frame guesses, to elaborate ideas simply for the sake of going through the meaningless process of seeing whether or not they agree with a truth already known.[2]

This alleged defect of the correspondence theory leads Dewey to say:

I hope this result may at least induce us to consider the other point of view; the notion that we do not have ideas separate from facts, which we proceed to compare one with the other, but that the (undoubted) distinction between idea and fact is itself logical, brought about by and within logical processes.[3]

It must be confessed that the terms "idea" and "fact" in this paper of Dewey's are quite baffling. Rather than attempt to extract a precise meaning for them, I shall, instead, present some of Dewey's more difficult words. Perhaps the reader will be able to detect a clear sense of Dewey's intent.

In early childhood, Dewey says, there is no distinction between ideas and facts.

[The child] does not recognize its ideas *as* ideas, but it at once projects them into the outer realm. . . . Suggest an idea to a baby by saying some word which he recognizes, the name of a known object or person, and the baby looks around him to see that object. A child's mind is like an animal's; it is intensely practical. Ideas, as such, do not appeal to it. The thing, the action is what the child is after.[4]

What happens, Dewey asks, to break up "this primitive intellectual innocency; this immediate transformation of

---

[2] *Ibid.*, p. 2225.   [3] *Ibid.*, p. 2226.   [4] *Ibid.*, p. 2226.

idea into fact"? Dewey's hypothesis is that disappointment, discovery of some ideas which have no factual counterparts, causes this. For instance, the baby may hear the word "papa," look around him, and not see his father. "Probably, at first, the new idea, what he actually sees, simply expels the other idea." As yet, Dewey thinks, "contradictions" are not perceived. "But there is at least the shock of unrealized expectation, and the feeling of the necessary adjustment to the new idea." But "as the mind's power of holding its ideas fixed becomes greater, the new idea will not simply drive out the other, substituting itself for it, but will struggle with it for the possession of the mind." Here, of course, are the beginnings of Dewey's doctrine of conflict and tension as the origin of thought. We have a "struggle," according to Dewey, between the "actual idea" and "the idea which the mind is endeavoring to project into actuality." This struggle, Dewey holds, leads the mind "to the hitherto unentertained recognition of an idea as only ideal, as a mere idea." [5]

There is, then, a distinction between two kinds of ideas. "The mind learns through the contradictions existing between its ideas, that not all can be projected as facts; some must be dismissed as false, or, at least, retained only tentatively as *possible* facts." Then Dewey says: "It is the tentative holding of an idea which constitutes the logical distinction of idea and fact. The fact is the idea which nothing contradicts, which harmonizes with other ideas, which allows the mind free play and economic movement." [6] There are ideas which are facts and ideas which are not facts. This, I suppose, is what is meant by saying that the distinction between idea and fact is made within the logical process.

Throughout this article Dewey strives to establish some kind of bridge between ideas and facts. And even though the language is difficult and the reasoning carried on with

[5] *Ibid.,* p. 2226.   [6] *Ibid.,* p. 2227.

idealist assumptions, the results would be accepted by Dewey today. In other words, the article, like most of Dewey's articles in the early nineties, has a prophetic character amid all its unclarity. Consider the following statement on scientific hypothesis:

The mind frames a hypothesis or theory, because it is dissatisfied with its present (or rather former) judgments. The ideas which it has formerly taken to be facts, it has come to look upon with suspicion. The hypothesis is an idea which is supposed to be fact, or at least, be nearer fact than previous ideas. But, till it can be verified, it is held only tentatively, and this holding may be of all degrees of comparative assurance, from a mere suggestion or question to a well-defined theory. The process of transforming the hypothesis, or idea entertained tentatively, into a fact, or idea held definitely, is verification. We saw at the outset the difficulties which beset the ordinary crude notion of verification, that which considers it as a process of comparing ready-made ideas with ready-made facts; let us see how our present notion meets these difficulties.[7]

Dewey goes on to urge that the facts are not a fixed, rigid something. Facts get transformed by theory just as theories are changed in the light of facts. The idea or theory is said to be tentative and pliable, "and must be bent to fit the facts"; the facts are said to be "elastic to the touch of theory." It follows from this conception of theory and fact "that there is no other test of a theory than . . . its ability to work, to organize facts." [8]

Despite the appearance of statements like the above that theories are tested by determining whether they work and also that concepts are modes of construction, it cannot be said that Dewey was an instrumentalist in 1890. Not that we shall ever be able to put a finger on the exact moment when he steps out of idealism into his present position; but we do know that Dewey was at that very time explicitly praising and defending Hegel's logical theory. Of course, we

[7] *Ibid.*, p. 2227.   [8] *Ibid.*, p. 2227.

might ask whether Dewey was an "instrumental Hegelian" at this time, and indeed this might be the best way to describe him during this transitional period. Dewey has said the following, in retrospect, of this period in his career:

With respect to more technically philosophical matters, the Hegelian emphasis upon continuity and the function of conflict persisted on empirical grounds after my earlier confidence in dialectic had given way to scepticism. There was a period extending into my earlier years at Chicago when, in connection with a seminar in Hegel's Logic, I tried reinterpreting his categories in terms of "readjustment" and "reconstruction." Gradually I came to realize that what the principles actually stood for could be better understood and stated when completely emancipated from Hegelian garb.[9]

The other ground for saying that Dewey was an "instrumental Hegelian" at that time was that he named his own philosophy "experimental idealism" in 1894.[10] The most stalwart defense of Hegel which Dewey has ever made also appeared during this period. In 1891 he published a paper [11] in which he referred to Hegel as "the quintessence of the scientific spirit."

Dewey begins the paper in the manner of a good Hegelian by pointing to what he calls a "contradiction" in the intellectual life of the time. On the one hand he sees an "enormous development of science," as a result of which, he says, one would expect intelligence to have confidence in itself, in its ability to solve problems of everyday life. But, he observes, instead of using the methods of science to guide life, scientific men deride any attempt to apply their methods to its problems.[12] This lack of confidence in scientific method, Dewey thinks, is due to the absence

---

[9] Schilpp, p. 18.   [10] *The Study of Ethics; a Syllabus*, p. 43.
[11] "The Present Position of Logical Theory," *Monist*, II, 1–17.
[12] Dewey says "Such a typical representative of modern science as Mr. Huxley virtually laughs to scorn the suggestion of Mr. Frederic Harrison that science should or could become so organized as to give any support, any authoritative stay to life." *Ibid.*, p. 1.

of an adequate logical theory. If there were a correct "synopsis of the methods and typical forms of intelligence" [13] available, "science and scientific men would be conscious of themselves, and would be confident of their work and attitude." [14] If there were a consistent, detailed account of the methods of science, these methods could be used in moral and social and political fields. Instead, Dewey found only confusion. His purpose in this paper was to describe the different elements that combined to form the confusion and to suggest a way out. [15]

"The especial problem of logic as the theory of scientific method," says Dewey, "is the relation of fact and thought to each other, of reality and thought." Fact "is the subject-matter under investigation, under consideration; it is that which we are trying to make out." Thought "means to logic what it means to science: method." [16] Now whatever "method" means, and its meaning has not emerged too clearly, it does not refer to any subjective process. Method

[13] *Ibid.*, pp. 1–2.   [14] *Ibid.*, p. 2.

[15] The title of Dewey's paper is very similar to the title of Andrew Seth's inaugural lecture at the University of Edinburgh, published in the same year—1891. Seth's lecture was called "The Present Position of the Philosophical Sciences." Not only were the titles similar, but the contents were, too.

Seth's comments on logic are of particular interest. He says: "Logic I will pass over lightly—almost with a word—because . . . its discussions are . . . technical in character . . . if we penetrate beneath the surface and examine the foundations on which it rests, we are immediately involved in difficult questions of general philosophy; and it becomes impossible to maintain a rigid distinction between Logic and Epistemology and Metaphysics. For that reason the very conception or definition of the science has long been matter of keen debate, and at present the aspect of things is confessedly chaotic. The activity, however, in the higher theory of logic has of late been great both in this country and in Germany. I need only refer to the important treaties of Lotze, Sigwart, and Wundt in Germany, and of Bradley and Bosanquet in this country, not to speak of the more distinctively English work of Jevons, Venn and others. The chaos, moreover, if at first bewildering, is not of the kind which should be disheartening to the serious student. It is the kind which portends and accompanies growth, and bears in it the promise of future order."

[16] "The Present Position of Logical Theory," *Monist*, II, p. 2.

is a way of handling subject matter. You can know that another man is thinking, just as you can know that he is building a house. The result has a twofold significance. It helps
Dewey steer through British dualism on the one hand and
the Hegelian *identification* of thought and subject matter.
Yet despite the veering from Hegel in doctrine, Dewey
qualifies his distinction between thought and subject matter
in a Hegelian manner. He says: "It is presupposed here that
there is some sort of fruitful and intrinsic connection of
fact and thought; that thinking, in short, is nothing but the
fact in its process of translation from brute impression to
lucent meaning." [17] This "intrinsic connection" between
fact and thought is the descendant of the "organic and internal relation" of Hegel and Morris. It is the residuum of
Hegel in Dewey, a sign of his admitted tendency to talk at
that time in Hegelian terms. But Dewey was self-conscious
about this contact with Hegelianism, for after having asserted this intrinsic connection between fact and thought,
he turns to his audience and lashes out at his opponents.
"But the moment such a presupposition is stated ninety-
nine persons out of a hundred think we have plunged, *ex
abrupto,* from the certainty of science into the cloudland of
metaphysic." This leads Dewey to summarize the position
of logic in 1891 as follows: "It is that any attempt to state,
in general, or to work out, in detail, the principle of the
intrinsic and fruitful relation of fact and thought which
science, without conscious reflection, constantly employs
in practice, seems 'metaphysical' or even absurd. Why is
this?" [18]

Dewey answers his own question:

The chief cause is that superstition which still holds enthralled
so much of modern thought—I mean formal logic. And if this
seems like applying a hard name to what, at best and at worst,

[17] *Ibid.,* pp. 2–3.   [18] *Ibid.,* p. 3.

is only an intellectual gymnastic, I can only say that formal logic seems to me to be, at present, *fons et origo malorum* in philosophy.[19]

For the first time Dewey now gives us a lengthy critique of formal logic. In his article on Venn, Mansel and Hamilton were assumed to be typical formal logicians. Now he chooses more contemporary (that is, contemporary to himself in 1891) examples—Jevons, in his *Elementary Lessons in Logic,* and Stock, the author of *Deductive Logic.*

Nowhere in his early attacks on formal logic does Dewey attack the science itself, that is, nowhere does he consider the laws of logic and criticize them in detail. In fact he says "nobody now takes the technical subject of formal logic very seriously—unless here and there some belated 'professor.'" It is not formal logic the science with which Dewey is concerned in these writings; rather it is "the conception of thought which is at the bottom of formal logic." For this conception of thought, according to the Dewey of 1891, "dominates the *Zeitgeist,* and regulates the doctrine and the method of all those who draw their inspiration from the *Zeitgeist.*" [20] Dewey summarizes the formal logician's idea of thought. For the formal logician, he says, thought "is a faculty or an entity existing in the mind apart from the facts, and . . . it has its own fixed forms, with which facts have nothing to do—except in so far as they pass under the yoke." [21]

---

[19] *Ibid.,* p. 3.   [20] *Ibid.,* p. 3.

[21] *Ibid.,* p. 3. Green, in his discussion of the formal logicians, makes similar allegations. He says: "With them logic is the science, not of the method of knowledge . . . but of those 'forms of thought' in conforming to which we think *correctly,* but in a way that contributes nothing to knowledge or truth. This view goes on the supposition that while, as all agree, knowledge has to do with real objects, there are processes of thought which do not affect and are not affected by such objects." (*Works,* II, 160.) But Green was fairly clear about distinguishing the formal, deductive laws presented by Mansel and Hamilton, from the speculations they made concerning thought. He was primarily concerned with criticizing the latter. Nevertheless he thought little of deductive logic too. For him its value was a minor

There were, then, two aspects of the position of the formal logicians—Mansel and Hamilton—that came under attack. Dewey and Green dismissed the formal, technical aspect as trivial and useless. They also opposed the statements made by these formal logicians on the nature of thought. The latter side of Mansel and Hamilton drew their heaviest fire. Although Mansel, for instance, distinguished both elements in his work, he believed they were inextricably bound up with each other. Logic, he said, was first of all a constructive and critical science. The pure formal logician inquires about the forms of reasoning (*barbara, celarent,* etc.) and also examines the reasoning of this or that person in order to determine its validity. This was the sense in which logic was a practical science; it represented the more innocuous aspects of the formalists' thought, according to the idealists. But Mansel and Hamilton were not content to occupy themselves only with purely formal logic. Mansel, for instance, says:

In order therefore [*sic*] to the right appreciation of any given system of logic, it becomes necessary to ask, what is the actual nature of thought as an operation, to what laws is it subject, and to what extent are they efficient? . . . Is the mind capable of other operations besides those of thought; and are there other kinds of mental rectitude besides that which results from the conformity of thought to its own laws? Do the several mental faculties act in the pursuit of truth conjointly or separately? [22]

"practical" one, it merely furnished us with rules "for securing consistency in the interpretation and application of general terms." (*Ibid.,* p. 161.) It represented, Green said, "neither a method of arriving at knowledge nor the system of ideas which constitutes the known world . . . but is merely of use for analyzing what is involved in conceded general propositions." (*Ibid.,* p. 160.) Green believed that its chief use lay in forensic and theological disputation, where "the object of argument is generally conviction of inconsistency." He even went further and said "The modern mind, in the effort to know the truth about nature itself, discards it [deductive logic]. Descartes, Spinoza, Leibniz (!) move in as complete freedom from it as Bacon or Newton." (*Ibid.,* p. 161.)

[22] *Prolegomena Logica,* pp. 18–19.

Mansel was conscious of the difference of these two do-
mains—so much so that he said of the nonformal side of
his work, "This inquiry does not, strictly speaking, fall
within the province of Logic itself . . . In relation to these
and similar questions, Logic is subordinate to *Psychology.*"
For this reason the book, *Prolegomena Logica,* was intended
"as an exposition of Psychology in relation to Logic, con-
taining such portions of the former as are absolutely necessary to the vindication and even to the understanding to
the latter." [23] Now it was this psychology, which Mansel
thought absolutely necessary to the understanding and
vindication of formal logic, that was the object of Dewey's
attack. It was the theory of thought expounded by one
school of formal logicians as the necessary adjunct of formal
logic that stirred Dewey's earliest opposition to formal logic.
The indiscriminate character of this opposition may best
be seen in his examination of certain passages of Jevons'
Elementary Lessons in Logic.

Dewey quotes the following statement by Jevons as typically formalist: "Just as we thus familiarly recognize the
difference of form and substance in common tangible things,
so we may observe in logic, that the form of an argument
is one thing, quite distinct from the various subjects of
matter which may be treated in that form." [24] This passage
elicits the following remark by Dewey:

It is assumed, in fine, that thought has a nature of its own independent of facts or subject matter; that this thought, *per se,*
has certain forms, and that these forms are not forms which the
facts themselves take, varying with the facts, but are rigid
frames, into which the facts are to be set.[25]

This is hardly the result of a fair reading of Jevons. First
of all, Jevons, as an inspection of the pages Dewey refers to

[23] *Ibid.,* Preface, p. iv.
[24] See Jevons, *op. cit.,* p. 5, and "The Present Position of Logical Theory,"
Monist, II, pp. 3–4.
[25] "The Present Position of Logical Theory," *Monist,* II, p. 4.

reveals, is not talking about all inference; he is talking about necessary inference. And he is simply trying to make the point that the argument "if London is identical with The Metropolis and The Metropolis is identical with the most populous city in Great Britain, then London is identical with the most populous city in Great Britain" is an argument which is valid in virtue of its form. In short, that the above conditional statement is true because the relation of identity is transitive and that the reasoning would still be valid if the three expressions "London," "the Metropolis," and "the most populous city in Great Britain" were respectively replaced by names of any three individual things. This is something which would be denied by very few contemporary mathematical logicians and could be maintained without involving one in any Kantian views of thought. The validity of Jevons' illustrative argument could be gathered on purely logical grounds, because the statement that identity is a transitive relation is logically true, that is, its truth depends only on the meaning of logical terms like "for every," "if-then," "and," and "is identical with." [26] In saying that the form of an argument is distinct from the various arguments which have the given form Jevons was hardly maintaining anything that could justify Dewey's attack.

Jevons, in the passage Dewey refers to at least, was restricting himself to arguments expressible as special cases of logical laws. Consequently, to charge him with holding that thought in general is carried on in this way was hardly fair. Jevons would have been one of the first to admit that there are other instances of thought or inference which are not expressible as special cases of logical law. Every inference made in accordance with some law of physics would fall into this latter category. In fact, only one year earlier

[26] See W. V. Quine, *Mathematical Logic*, New York, Norton, 1940, pp. 1–2, and Alfred Tarski, *Introduction to Logic*, New York, Oxford, 1941, pp. 120–130.

Dewey himself had said, in his review of Venn, that Jevons was one of those logicians who recognized the importance of a methodology of empirical science and did not insist that all thought was purely formal. Moreover, even Mansel, as a reading of the *Prolegomena Logica* shows, did not believe that the laws of identity, noncontradiction, and excluded middle were the only kinds of law of thought. They were laws of "pure" thought and in the same class as Jevons' law above, to the effect that identity is a transitive relation. In the sixth and seventh chapters of the *Prolegomena* Mansel labors the point concerning the difference between "formal," or "pure," thought and "mixed," or "material," thought. The latter, he insists, must be studied by the psychologist.

The place in which the formal logicians were most vulnerable was just where they did present their psychology. It was against this that Dewey was reacting. And he reacted so strongly that he dismissed all the work of the formal logicians. Thus he says categorically: "Formal thought, with its formulae for simply unfolding a given material, is of no use in science." [27] In his zeal to reject every claim of formal logic and to propagandize for the building of an instrumental logic or methodology of empirical science he declared deductive logic useless.[28] But one does not have to reject formal logic in order to maintain that it is not

27 *Monist*, II, p. 8.

28 It is not completely clear whether Dewey is saying here that the sciences do not use deduction or that they simply do not consciously apply laws of logic in their reasoning. The former is obviously untrue, the latter is true. But even if the latter is true, i. e., even if it is true that most scientists operate without knowing the laws of logic in great detail, it would not follow that formal logic is useless. There is, of course, also the fact that Dewey meant by formal logic, the Aristotelian logic, which, in so far as it is not employed extensively in advanced deductive sciences, is comparatively useless. But this latter fact would not be sufficient to condemn all formal logic, including, as this does, the vast generalization of formal logic represented by modern mathematical logic.

an empirical account of thought as it is carried on by scientists. It was just the recognition of this fact that impelled the English logicians of the latter part of the nineteenth century to write their inductive logics. Jevons not only contributed to mathematical logic but also wrote his *Principles of Science;* Venn wrote about empirical logic as well as symbolic logic.

Despite these attempts on the part of the empirical logicians to formulate a methodolgy of science, Dewey opposed them. For not only did he believe, as we have seen, that their formal logic was useless, but he also held that their empirical logic made no advance. "Empirical logic," he says, "virtually continues the conception of thought as in itself empty and formal, which characterizes scholastic logic." [29] Mill, who hardly had the interest in formal logic that his disciple Venn had, is none the less a formalist. Mill, Dewey points out, defended the syllogism and in this respect was at one with the scholastics. The empiricists differed from the scholastics only concerning the way in which they believed the major premise is reached. The scholastics, according to Dewey, believed we arrive at the material premises by intuition, whereas the school of Mill and Locke appealed to experience. He grants that in this respect empiricism is preferable to scholasticism. But, and here we come to the central accusation, empiricism, even in its description of how the premises for formal syllogistic thought are reached, is formalist in approach according to Dewey. Because:

Thought being confined to the rigid framework in which the material is manipulated after being obtained, is excluded from all share in the gathering of material. The result is that this material, having no thought-side, shrinks into a more or less accidental association of more or less shifting and transitory states.[30]

[29] *Ibid.,* p. 5.   [30] *Ibid.,* p. 7.

Because the empiricist logicians did not surrender their belief that the materials for proof were not gathered by thought, they remained for Dewey formalists beneath the skin. They were, Morris would have said, "mechanical" in approach, and only a conversion to Hegelianism could have saved them.

Only transcendental logic could furnish what Dewey sought in 1891. True, it was "a co-worker with the spirit and intent of 'inductive logic.' " But it differed crucially from inductive logic; "It has simply gone a step further . . . and thrown overboard once for all the scholastic idea of thought." [31]

Dewey was relatively defensive about his acceptance of transcendental logic. For the first time he felt obliged to "explain" his idealism. He was at the stage when the attacks on idealism began to affect him considerably. Therefore, to his statement that transcendental logic and inductive logic were partners in the attempt to describe the method of science he added that he was "well aware that inductive logic is usually conceived as specifically 'scientific,' while the transcendental movement is regarded as the especial foe of science—as a belated attempt to restore an *a priori* scholasticism, and to find a scheme for evolving truth out of pure thought." [32] This view, he says, follows from a misconstrual of idealist thought. And this in turn is connected with the fact that people stop at Kant and do not go on to read Hegel. For Kant, Dewey thinks, is far more transcendental in the usual sense. That is, he says, the Kantian philosophy "is more *a priori*, more given to emphasizing some special thought-power—than the Hegelian." [33] Kant begins with the scholastic view, according to which thought exists apart from fact. Kant's analysis of knowledge, Dewey says, led him to the conclusion that there were two separate factors—the a priori and the a posteriori; he thus postu-

---

[31] *Ibid.,* p. 9.   [32] *Ibid.,* p. 9.   [33] *Ibid.,* p. 10.

lates formal thought on the one hand and unrelated sensations on the other.

Kant must now piece together his two separated factors. Sensation, unrelated manifold of sensation is *there,* thought, isolated,
analytic thought, is *here.* Neither is knowledge in itself. What
more natural than to put them together, and hold that knowledge is the union of a matter or stuff of sensations atomic in
themselves, on one hand, and a form, or regulating principle of
thought, empty in itself, on the other. We have two elements,
both existing in isolation, and yet both useless for all purposes
of knowledge. Combine them, and presto, there is science.[34]

In Hegel, Dewey finds no such conception of thought
and of the a priori. Although Kant, Dewey points out,
formulated the conception of thought as objective, he meant
that thought, subjective in itself, becomes objective when
it is synthetic of a given sense manifold. But,

When Hegel calls thought objective he means just what he says:
that there is no special, apart faculty of thought belonging to
and operated by a mind existing separate from the outer world.
What Hegel means by objective thought is the meaning, the
significance of the fact itself; and by methods of thought he
understands simply the processes in which meaning of this fact
is involved.[35]

For this reason Dewey believes that Hegel represents "the
quintessence of the scientific spirit." He indicates at the
same time that he is not referring to any of Hegel's specific
scientific theories or to any of the particular meanings Hegel
assigned to reality. His chief point is that Hegel conceived
of reality as a connected system.[36]

The failure to go on to Hegel, it will be recalled, is given
as one reason for the misunderstandings of transcendental
logic. But there is another reason, according to Dewey, associated with the history of science. He says that "the ration-
ality of fact had not been sufficiently realized in detail in
the early decades of the century to admit of the 'transcen-

dental' movement being otherwise than misunderstood."
Science at that time was too rudimentary, and therefore
Hegel was born too early. "On account of this lack of scientific discovery and application, the world presented itself
to man's consciousness as a blank, or at least as only *stuff*
for meaning, and not as itself significant." The result was
that Hegel was interpreted subjectively.

The difficulties in the way of conceiving a world, upon which
science had not yet expended its energies in detail, as an organism of significant relations and bearings were so great, that
Hegel's attempt to point out these significant types and functions as immanent in reality was inevitably misconstrued as an
attempt, on Hegel's part, to prove that a system of purely "subjective" thoughts could somehow be so manipulated as to give
objectively valid results.[37]

It follows that "Hegel . . . anticipated somewhat the actual outcome of the scientific movement," just as Leibniz,
according to Dewey, anticipated the importance of organic
unity before the rise of biological science. Science simply
illustrated or found out what Hegel and Leibniz knew long
before that time. Science came simply to make it easier for
people to recognize the truth in idealism. Because no matter
how much Hegel urged that fact was significant and that
thought was not a separate faculty mechanically related to
fact, "yet to man this objective significance cannot be real
till he has made it *out* in the details of scientific procedure,
and *made* it applied in science and invention." [38]

Finite man is still looked upon by Dewey as patiently
"making out" what has already been instituted by objective
mind. This paper of 1891 still defends Hegel. But it is the
last great defense of Hegel to be found in Dewey's logical
writings. Between 1891 and 1900 he wrote very little on
logic. But in 1900 the article "Some Stages of Logical
Thought" announced the death of formal, inductive, and

transcendental logic. A new one—the Deweyan logic—is offered. The road to this position is a long one, and as the dearth of logical papers between 1891 and 1900 may indicate, it was reached as a result of work in many other fields —ethics, psychology, and education.

CHAPTER SEVEN

FROM ETHICAL IDEALISM TO SOCIAL PSYCHOLOGY

Although Dewey's ethical writings were the first to indicate a turn away from idealism, it is not true to say that all his ethical writings were anti-idealist in approach. The papers "Ethics and Physical Science" [1] and "The Ethics of Democracy," [2] published in 1887 and 1888, respectively, were totally idealist in outlook, and so it cannot be said that Dewey was an idealist who suddenly became interested in ethics and whose ethical investigations forced him to see the error of his idealist ways. Yet it is accurate to say that his most explicit criticisms of idealism first appeared in his discussions of ethical questions, particularly in his *The Study of Ethics: a Syllabus,* which appeared in 1894.

ETHICAL IDEALISM

Between 1882 and 1890 the two papers mentioned above were his only two extended studies of ethical subjects. As might have been expected, both stated the doctrine of Green, Morris, and Hegel with little alteration.

The paper on ethics and physical science, a critique of evolutionary ethics, draws heavily on Morris [3] and on

[1] *Andover Review,* VII, 573–591.

[2] This was a lecture delivered at the University of Michigan and published as one of the University of Michigan "Philosophical Papers," Second Series, No. 1.

[3] We have already observed Morris' attitude to Spencer. This appears in the chapter on Spencer in *British Thought and Thinkers* and also throughout *Philosophy and Christianity;* in the latter see pp. 283–284 in particular.

Green [4] for its ammunition. Its major point is a radical distinction between "what-is" and "what-ought-to-be"; values and ethical judgments are sharply separated from physical existences and the laws of physical science. Therefore, Herbert Spencer, as the alleged advocate of ethics as a physical science, is the object of Dewey's attack. After stating the "evolutionary" view at length, Dewey says:

In spite of the vigor and ardor with which these ideas are urged, some of us, at least, remain unmoved. We believe that the cause of theology and morals is one, and that whatever banished God from the heart of things, with the same edict excludes the ideal, the ethical from the life of man. [5]

This banishment of God from the heart of things was the banishment of Green's "spiritual principle" from nature. It followed from Spencer's "purely physical" interpretation of reality, according to which reality is not ideal, that is, not alive with universal spirit. This was the argument from the existence of the universal mind.

There was also the argument which was simply based on an analysis of human, moral action. Dewey argued that conscious behavior had two characteristics which were "incongruous with and contradictory to the principles which a purely physical philosophy . . . must insist upon." [6] These characteristics were (1) activity for an end or toward an ideal, (2) activity from choice. They could not be defined in terms of purely physical concepts, Dewey maintained. Therefore, since ethics involved them essentially, ethics involved a reference beyond physical science. It must be observed that in projecting this double-barreled argument against Spencer, Dewey repeats his early use of two minds —the absolute and the individual. The attack derived from the existence of an absolute is gradually dropped, as we have emphasized. But the argument from the existence of an individual mind, which is essentially an empirical argu-

---

[4] *Works*, I, 373–441.   [5] *Andover Review*, VII, 576.   [6] *Ibid.*, p. 577.

ment to the effect that purposive behavior needs more than physics for its description, is amplified and fortified later on.

"The Ethics of Democracy" is even more strikingly dominated by Hegelian organicism. In it Sir Henry Maine is criticized for failing to realize that society is an organism and that government is an expression of its organic nature. The organic theory, to which Dewey subscribed, implied, on the contrary, "that men are not isolated non-social atoms, but are men only when in intrinsic relations to men" [7] and that democracy as a form of society "not only does have, but must have, a common will; for it is this unity of will which makes it an organism." [8]

These two papers form the bulk of Dewey's writings on ethics before the nineties. They share an opposition to empiricism, but they are different in one interesting respect. Whereas the paper on ethics and physical science is devoted to separating value from fact, the one on ethics and democracy tends to emphasize the ideal, rational character of fact. The ambivalence is the ambivalence of Hegel, who attacked the "mechanical" approach to human problems and also called the real rational. When he attacked the mechanical approach, he made way for the growth of social science and the emphasis upon process; when he called the real "rational," he made way for the right Hegelians. Soon, however, the former, the tendency that culminates in his social psychology, prevails; signs of right Hegelianism leave forever.

THE IMPENDING BREAK

In 1889 Dewey described the courses in ethics at Michigan for the academic year 1889–1890.[9] In his description of one course in ethics he practically outlines his first book on ethics, *Outlines of a Critical Theory of Ethics*, which ap-

---

[7] University of Michigan, "Philosophical Papers," Second Series, No. 1, p. 6.

[8] *Ibid.*, p. 7.   [9] *The Ethical Record*, II, 145–148.

peared in 1891. The course, like the book, was divided into three sections. "The first is the theory of the moral ideal; the second, the Objective Moral World; the third, the Concrete Moral Life of the Individual." The aim of the first part, Dewey tells us, was to discover the ethical ideal, or to answer the question "What is the chief end of man?" After critically examining hedonism, the evolutionary extension of it in Spencer, utilitarianism, the theological ethics of Paley, and Kantian ethics, "it is finally concluded that only the theory that the ideal of conduct is realization of personality answers all the demands of the problem." [10] This, we know, was the keystone of Green's ethical theory.

It was just at about this time that the most significant instrumentalist murmurs began to appear in Dewey's philosophy. In 1890 he had written his review of Venn's logic, in which he spoke about the test of theories being their capacity to work. But we also know that during this same year he called Caird's book on Kant the best book on philosophy in English; 1890, then, was a critical year in Dewey's development, a year in which he extolled Hegelianism and announced an early version of the pragmatist theory of truth. The manner in which he held on to both is illustrated by the fact that what he meant by a "working" theory was a theory that organized facts. In other words, the pragmatist elements in Dewey's thought were expressed within the framework of organicism. The same is true, we know, of his article "The Present Position of Logical Theory."

The *Outlines* contain more detailed evidence of Dewey's shifting outlook. They even suggest the way in which idealist organicism gives way to the earliest traces of instrumentalism. A letter written by Dewey to William James in 1903 lends confirmation to the hypothesis that the *Outlines,* which appeared in 1891, marked a crucial point in Dewey's development. Dewey was replying to a question

[10] *Ibid.,* p. 146.

James had asked concerning the origin of the "new school
of thought" at Chicago. He said: "As for the standpoint,
we have all been at work at it for about twelve years." [11]
And twelve years before 1903 was exactly the year in which
the *Outlines* appeared. The *Outlines*, however, were still
predominantly idealist in character; they contained only
glimmerings of the impending break with the doctrine of
Morris, the English idealists, and Hegel. The ideal of conduct is said to be the realization of personality or self; moral
life is growth in freedom "as the individual finds and con-
forms to the law of his social placing." [12] The books most
heavily relied upon, those which furnish the "backbone"
of his theory, are, according to Dewey: Green's *Prolegomena
to Ethics*, Bradley's *Ethical Studies*, E. Caird's *Social Philosophy of Comte*, and *Critical Philosophy of Kant*, and
Alexander's *Moral Order and Progress*.

In addition to these general, pervasive influences on his
ethics there was one to which reference is rarely made. Even
Miss Dewey, in her excellent biographical sketch, fails to
mention the name of Franklin Ford. Now, in the Preface to
the *Outlines*, after mentioning the professional philosophers
who had influenced him, Dewey proceeds to describe the
leading ideas of the book. These are, he said:

the idea of desire as the ideal activity in contrast with actual
possession . . . the analysis of individuality into function including capacity and environment . . . the treatment of the
social bearings of science and art (a point concerning which I
am indebted to my friend, Mr. Franklin Ford).

Who was Franklin Ford? We have a letter from Dewey to
James in which Ford's work and relation to Dewey's *Outlines* are discussed in some detail. Dewey says,

I should say that there is something back (and something ahead)
of whatever freedom of sight and treatment there is in my ethics.

[11] See Perry, *The Thought and Character of William James*, II, 520.
[12] *Outlines of a Critical Theory of Ethics*, p. vii.

I got it from Franklin Ford to whom I refer in the Preface. By some sort of instinct, and by the impossibility of my doing anything in particular, I was led into philosophy and into "idealism,"—i. e., the conception of some organism comprehending both man's thought and the external world. Ford, who was a newspaper man (formerly Editor of Bradstreet's in New York) with no previous philosophical training, had been led by his newspaper experience to study as a practical question the social bearings of intelligence and its distribution. That is to say, he was on a paper and wanted to inquire. The paper would not let him: the more he was stopped, the more his desire to inquire was aroused, until finally he was drawn into a study of the whole matter—especially as he found that it was not any one newspaper, but rather the social structure, which prevented freedom of inquiry. Well, he identified the question of inquiry with, in philosophical terms, the question of the relation of intelligence to the objective world—is the former free to move in relation to the latter or not? So he studied out the following questions: (1) The conditions and effects of the distribution of intelligence especially with reference to inquiry, or the selling of truth as a business; (2) the present (or past) hindrances to its free play, in the way of class interests; or (3) the present conditions in the railway, telegraph, etc., for effectively securing the freedom of intelligence, that is, its movement in the world of social fact; and (4) the resulting social organization. That is, with inquiry as a *business,* the selling of truth for money, the *whole* would have a representative as well as the various classes —a representative whose belly interest, moreover, is identical with its truth interest. Now I am simply reducing what was a wonderful personal experience to a crude bit of cataloguing, but I hope it may arouse your interest in the man and his work.[18]

The work of Ford is fascinating not only in its own right but all the more so because of its impact on Dewey. Dewey says,

What I have got out of it is, first, the perception of the true or practical bearing of idealism—that philosophy has been the assertion of the unity of intelligence and the external world *in idea* or subjectively, while if true in idea it must finally secure the conditions of its objective expression. And secondly, I be-

18 Perry, *op. cit.,* p. 518.

lieve that a tremendous movement is impending, when the intellectual forces which have been gathering since the Renascence and Reformation, shall demand complete free movement, and, by getting their physical leverage in the telegraph and printing press, shall, through free inquiry in a centralized way, demand the authority of all other so-called authorities. It is impossible to convey what I mean in a page or two, but, as I am all the more anxious to see you and talk with you on this very account, I hope I may not have made you suspicious of me. I shall have with me in the summer a number of Ford's own writings which will convey it in an orderly and rational way. I do not think that anyone who, like yourself, has the intellectual interest developed, the thirst for inquiry with no special interest or precept or church or philosophy to "save," can fail of being interested both in his theoretical discovery and in his practical project.[14]

Coming in 1891, this letter, I believe, presages Dewey's break with idealism, despite his statement that Ford's work showed the practical bearings of idealism. The admission that intelligence and the world are unified only in idea suggests doubt concerning the doctrine that the real is rational. The world is no longer "logical through and through." Potentially, the world is one that may be controlled by intelligence. This is the first great relaxation of Dewey's idealist fervor, the first serious questioning of the universal mind. It also marks the beginning of Dewey's long crusade for the application of intelligence in social affairs, which expresses itself in his two short essays on Ernest Renan, written in 1892 and 1893. In them Dewey compares the optimism of the *Future of Science* of 1848 and the surrender to reaction that appears in 1890. The early period attracts Dewey. For "Renan's faith in '48 was that science was to become universalized—universalized in its *range* by coming to include humanity as its subject matter; universalized in *application* by being made, as to its salient outcome the common possession of all men." [15]

14 *Ibid.*, pp. 518–519.   15 See Dewey, *Characters and Events*, I, 27.

Dewey points to the strength in Renan's early conception of science as a "social motor," his faith in a "wide distribution of intelligence as the basis of a scientifically controlled democracy." Here are some of the earliest statements by Dewey on the social function of science. Note that the phrase "distribution of intelligence" appears significantly in the letter to James on Franklin Ford.

Dewey's concern with the social function of intelligence permeated all his work at that time. It will be recalled that in "The Present Position of Logical Theory" he regretted the divorce between science and the world and that he believed this to be due to a misconception of the nature of science. If only there were competent methodologists who could point out the intrinsic relation between thought and the world, then science might be confidently applied to the world's problems. In a very short time this unity of world and thought is transformed by Dewey into a unity of practice and theory. The emphasis then is no longer put on a world constituted by the universal mind, whose meanings are to be deciphered by individuals. The concept of universal mind drops out. Dewey speaks of individuals who do not simply try to recapture what the absolute had previously installed, of individuals who must adjust and construct instruments which will help them solve their problems. They must unify their theory with practice, and this act of unification is not simply a repetition of earlier acts of the absolute.

It must be remembered, however, that in 1891 Dewey still holds to the belief that the unity of theory and practice is preordained "in idea," that the control which intelligence exerts over the world is simply a necessary development of a mysterious Absolute. Thus he says:

The intellectual movement of the last four or five centuries has resulted in an infinite specialization in methods, and in an immense accumulation of fact. It is quite true, since the diversity of fact and of method has not yet been brought to an organic unity, that their social bearing is not yet realized. But when the unity is attained (as attained it must be if there is a unity in the object of knowledge) it will pass into a corresponding unity of practice.[16]

It is not until the pragmatic elements in Dewey's philosophy become stronger that the universal self is completely discarded. This takes place in his attacks on his youthful idol, Green, in 1892 and 1893.

Green was mainly responsible for Dewey's belief that the ethical ideal was self-realization. Green's influence on Dewey's ethical thought was simply a special case of his general domination of all of Dewey's thought in the eighties. It was not until Dewey's review of Caird's book on Kant, so far as I have been able to discover, that Dewey leveled serious criticism against Green. In that review he said that Green "never . . . quite freed himself from the negative element in Kant—the idea that the regress from the world to self is an abstracting process, resulting in the notion of a spirit, *for* which indeed reality exists, but of which nothing in itself may be said." [17] This questioning of Green's conception of spirit or universal consciousness is a turning point in Dewey's attitude toward Green. Only the year before, in the same journal, Dewey offered no sharp criticism of Green's doctrine of the self, which he stated as follows: "These are the two fundamental positions of Green's constructive work: on one side an eternal self-consciousness, as involved in the reality of experience; on the other, human consciousness, a progressive reproduction of this divine consciousness." [18]

That the criticism of Green occurred in the review in which Dewey lavished praise on Caird is significant. He now thought that Caird was a Hegelian, but that Green, despite

[16] *Outlines,* p. 126.   [17] *Andover Review,* XIII (1890), 326.
[18] "The Philosophy of Thomas Hill Green," *Andover Review,* XI (1889), 344–345.

seeming evidence to the contrary, was really a Kantian. He says:

So far as I know it has not been pointed out that Green, while arguing against such [Kant's] separation of sense and reason, on the ground that we cannot know sense or desire at all except as determined by reason, yet practically repeats the dualism of Kant in slightly altered form. For the conception of action determined by the pure form of self, Green simply substitutes action determined by the self in its unity; for conduct determined by mere appetite, he substitutes conduct determined by the self in some particular aspect. The dualism between reason and sense is given up, indeed, but only to be replaced by a dualism between the end which would satisfy the self as a unity or whole, and that which satisfies itself in the particular circumstances of actual conduct. The end which would satisfy the self as unity is just as far from the end which satisfies the self in any special instance of action, as in Kant's system, the satisfaction of pure reason, is remote from the satisfaction of mere appetite. Indeed, we may go a step further, and say that the opposition is even more decided and intrinsic in Green than in Kant. It is at least conccivable, according to Kant, that in some happy moment action should take place from the motive of reason shorn of all sensuous content and thus be truly moral. But in no possible circumstance, according to Green, can action satisfy the whole self and thus be truly moral. In Kant the discrepancy between the force which appetite exercises, and the controlling force at the command of pure reason, is so great as to make very extraordinary the occurrence of a purely moral action; but at least there is no intrinsic impossibility in the conception, however heavy the odds against its actual happening. In Green, however, the thing is impossible by the very definition of morality. No thorough-going theory of total depravity ever made righteousness more impossible to natural man than Green makes it to a human being by the very constitution of his being.[19]

In his criticism of Green, Dewey was conscious of his break with his past and also conscious that he was not participating in "the refusal to subject certain ideas to unswerving analysis because of sympathy with the moral atmosphere

[19] *Philosophical Review*, I (1892), 597–598.

which bathes those ideas." [20] But his sympathy with that moral atmosphere was great, and therefore his attack on Green's ethic and metaphysic was dragged out. He continued to hammer away at his chains. In the next volume of *Philosophical Review* (1893) he published his paper "Self-Realization as the Moral Ideal." He points out that his previous paper had considered the ideal or divine consciousness of Green, whereas this one would discuss its reproduction or realization, that is, the individual self.

The notion which I wish to criticize is that of the self as a presupposed fixed schema or *outline,* while realization consists in the filling up of this *schema.* The notion which I would suggest as substitute is that of the self as always a concrete *specific* activity; and, *therefore, (to anticipate) of the identity of self and realization.*[21]

The next effect of these two papers is to drop the two entities he had postulated in the *Psychology,* the universal mind and the individual ego, where these are construed as hidden or trans-empirical. The former is dispensed with metaphysically; the latter is interpreted as a mode of individual behavior. For this reason, in his discussion "The Ego as Cause," [22] he rejects all views of the ego as "an efficient cause of volition." He says:

When one man says to another, "You did that and I shall hold you responsible for it," he means by his "you," not a metaphysical ego, but a definite individual—John Smith. Every step away from the concrete individual, John Smith, with his special aptitudes, habits, desires, ideas, and ignorances, every step toward an ego in general, means a weakening of the connection between the man and the act, and a release of the man from the responsibility of the act.[23]

This refusal to countenance any kind of metaphysical ego leads Dewey to criticize James in a footnote. There he makes

20 *Ibid.,* p. 608.   21 *Philosophical Review,* II, 653.
22 *Philosophical Review,* III, 337–341.   23 *Ibid.,* p. 340.

substantially the point he makes in an article on James written in 1940.[24] In the footnote he says:

It is strange that Professor James, who recognizes so far as knowledge is concerned the entire uselessness of an ego outside and behind, who indeed has given that theory the hardest knocks it has received from the psychological side (Vol. I, pp. 360–370), should feel bound to set up its correlate when he comes to deal with will. If the stream of thought can run itself in one case, the stream of conduct may administer itself in the other. Why should he deny to the transcendentalist ego in knowing a power which he claims for attention in acting? [25]

Concerning this criticism of James, Professor G. W. Allport has said: "So whole-hearted is his conversion to the functional position that Dewey accuses James of faint-heartedness." [26] Dewey now would out-James James. This is an ironic situation. For when Dewey's own *Psychology* appeared, James, writing to Croom Robertson, commented:

Dewey is out with a psychology which I have just received and but one-half read. I felt quite "enthused" at the first glance, hoping for something really fresh; but am sorely disappointed when I come to read. It's no use trying to mediate between the bare miraculous self and the concrete particulars of individual mental lives; and all that Dewey effects by so doing is to take all the edge and definiteness away from the particulars when it falls their turn to be treated.[27]

The cycle is completed in 1894. Dewey not only overtakes James, but passes him. This will appear in the *Syllabus* on ethics, another product of 1894, and is intimately linked with Dewey's growing interest in connecting ethics with the social sciences. By 1896 this is quite explicit. His review of D'Arcy's *A Short Study of Ethics* contains an attack on "The Metaphysical Method in Ethics" and concludes with a suggestion: "The results of Mr. D'Arcy's investigations

---

[24] "The Vanishing Subject in the Psychology of James," *Journal of Philosophy*, XXXVII, 589–599.

[25] *Philosophical Review*, III, 340n.   [26] Schilpp, p. 268.

[27] Quoted in Perry, *Thought and Character of William James*, II, 516.

whose aim is to find a metaphysical foundation for ethics seem to me to give at least negative support to the hypothesis that what ethical theory now needs is an adequate psychological and social method, not a metaphysical one." [28]

[28] *Psychological Review*, III (1896), 188.

CHAPTER EIGHT

EVOLUTION AND IDEALISM

In 1894, after the rejection of the empty universal self of Green and the transcendental individual self of James, Dewey published *The Study of Ethics: a Syllabus.* The immediate reason for its appearance was the exhaustion of the edition of his *Outlines.* But the *Syllabus,* Dewey insisted,[1] was in no sense a second edition of the previous book. On the contrary, it undertook "a thorough psychological examination of the process of active experience and a derivation from this analysis of the chief ethical types and crises," [2] a task, so far as Dewey knew, never before attempted.

The *Syllabus* breathes a completely new atmosphere. Immediately one realizes that the Dewey we know at present has at last made his appearance—and no longer in the costume of a routine idealist. The language of experiment, instruments, practice, and conflict, is already here, waiting restlessly to be permuted and combined and carried to the conclusions of the *Studies in Logical Theory.* In the very first chapter we meet the clipped syllabus lines: "Current antithesis between science and art not tenable . . . Science does not *teach* us to know; it is the knowing; art does not *teach* us to do, it is the doing." And obviously, if science is an art, knowing is a kind of art, a kind of doing. From now on old idealist contentions are either dropped or where re-

---

[1] *The Study of Ethics: a Syllabus,* Prefatory Note; this volume will be referred to as *Syllabus* hereafter.
[2] *Ibid.,* Prefatory Note.

tained, retained not in their Hegelian form, but revised and
bolstered by new naturalistic arguments.

EXPERIMENTAL IDEALISM

There is, of course, continuity with the past. For instance,
Dewey's theory of the norm in the *Outlines* has important
connections with his theory of the norm in the *Syllabus*. In
the *Outlines* Dewey says:

Three of the branches of philosophy may be called *normative,*
implying that they deal with some *norm, standard,* or end, esti-
mating the value of their respective subject matters as tested
by this end. These are Logic, dealing with the end Truth, and
the value of intellectual processes with respect to it; Aesthetics,
dealing with Beauty and the value of emotional conditions as
referred to it; and Ethics . . .

To this Dewey significantly adds, "But this norm in no case
comes from outside the subject matter; it is the subject matter considered in its totality." [3] The basis of this doctrine is
the conception of the norm as not cut off from the subject
matter. Its background was the idealistic belief in the objective existence of norms, which in turn was linked with a
belief in the immanence of the objective mind. This doctrine continues in the *Syllabus* despite the general shift
away from idealism. In the *Syllabus* Dewey says: "The completest possible interaction of an impulse with all other experiences, or the completest possible relation of an impulse
to the whole self constitutes the . . . moral value of an act."
In a footnote Dewey adds that the above "has important
bearings upon the subject of the *criterion* . . . the criterion always lies within, not without, the act. The criterion
is nothing but the completest possible view of the act." [4]
This continuity which exists between his last thoroughly
idealist book and the first book in which signs of experimentalism appear is a fundamental one. It might be said

[3] *Outlines,* pp. 1–2.   [4] *Syllabus,* p. 22.

that the conception of the criterion involved is one which may be traced through the *Studies in Logical Theory* and up to the *Logic*. It is the earliest statement of Dewey's attack on the theory of norms as introduced *ab extra*.

The basis for the opposition to the *ab extra* introduction of norms is vaguely formulated and is connected with a belief in the organic unity of fact and norm. This concept of organic unity presented a means of stating early versions of other doctrines of instrumentalism. In discussing the relation between the consequences of an act and the act itself, in the *Outlines*, Dewey says:

Just in the degree that any consequence is considered likely to result from an act, just in that degree it gets its moral value, for it becomes *part of the act* itself. The reason that in many cases we cannot judge of the morality of an intended act until we can judge its probable results, is that until we know of these results the action is a mere abstraction, having no content at all. *The conceived results constitute the content of the act to be performed.* They are not merely relevant to its morality, but *are* its moral quality. The question is whether any consequence is foreseen, conceived, or not.[5]

Here we have the view that the consequences of an act are part of the act, that is, organically connected with the act. And of course this has obvious connections with Dewey's later views on ethics and logic, in which no reference is made to a Hegelian organic unity.

The kind of continuity which exists between Dewey's early work and his later work simply illustrates the continuity between his idealism and his experimentalism. They share, as we have emphasized frequently, activism, organicism, and opposition to formalism and dualism. This is concretely shown by the fact that Dewey continued to call his philosophy "idealism" in 1894. But by this time it was a very special and new kind of idealism, for "experimental idealism" is Dewey's new label. What could be a more appropriate name for the type of philosophy Dewey accepted at the transitional point in his intellectual history—the point at which his idealism drifts into experimentalism? The retention of the word "idealism" is not simply a pious tribute to Green; it corresponded to the kind of revision of Green that Dewey thought he was performing.

The ethical ideal in Green's system is the complete realization in man of the universal self. According to Dewey self-realization is still the ideal, but it takes on a completely new significance. "The identity of agent and act has been our guiding principle," [6] Dewey says. Therefore the agent, or self, is no remote universal mind, nor is it some individual ego. It is simply a mode of the human being's behavior. The concept is never sharpened as much as it should have been, but enough to make clear what Dewey did *not* intend by the term "self." The term is thoroughly empirical according to Dewey's intention, and it is to be construed as meaning something like "social organism."

Social organisms take part in impulsive action, as all animals do, according to Dewey, and impulsive acts may be divided into two groups: "Some acts tend to narrow the self, to introduce friction into it, to weaken its power, and in various ways to *disintegrate* it, while other acts tend to expand, invigorate, and harmonize, and in general organize the self." The acts in the first group are called "right," those in the second, "wrong." Right behavior is that behavior which organizes, or has an integrating effect upon the individual. All those impulses which do not contribute to this total effect must be mediated, Dewey says. So the doctrine of self-realization, as Dewey interprets it, does not set up the blind expression of impulse as an ideal. Some impulses must be reconstructed. Concerning this mediation or reconstruction Dewey says:

[6] *Syllabus*, p. 73.

The first effect of every mediation of an impulse is to check or arrest that impulse. Reflection means postponement; it is delayed action. Through this delay the impulse is brought into connection with other impulses, habits, and experiences. Now if a due balance is kept, the result is that the original impulse is harmonized with the self, and when expressed, it realizes not only its own partial nature but that of the whole self. . . . The bad act is partial, the good organic.

The organicism, of course, is the link with Green. And therefore Dewey adds a kind of postscript to his analysis, saying:

The same idea is also expressed in the conception of "self-realization," provided this is understood in the sense of expressing the concrete capacity of an individual agent and not in the sense of filling the blank scheme of some undefined, purely general self.[7]

The latter interpretation, he says, is the view of Green and Bradley. It is the view he had so vehemently rejected in his farewell to Green. Nevertheless, although Dewey no longer considered himself a Greenian in 1894, it was Green who was his starting point. Although Green's conception of self-realization was ghostlike, it served a purpose. When it was revised and given content, it became Dewey's experimental idealism. Green's idealism stemmed the tide of atomism until Dewey could fight it in his own way. Again, as in his logical theory, Dewey's views spring from a renovated idealism.

ALFRED LLOYD'S DYNAMIC IDEALISM

The transformation Dewey was working on idealism in the nineties was not something isolated. Dewey was not the only one engaged in the attempt to build a new philosophy on the basis of the usable elements in idealism. In the 1903 letter to James in which he says that he had been working on his "standpoint" for about twelve years, he also says, "Lloyd and Mead were both at it in Ann Arbor ten years ago" and asks James, "Did you ever read Lloyd's *Dynamic Idealism?*"

The connection between Mead and Dewey is a subject of contemporary investigation. The recent posthumous publication of so much of Mead's work has stirred up considerable interest in his brand of pragmatism and its relations with Dewey's. But Alfred Lloyd goes unmentioned today, despite the fact that he published much more than Mead did in these early years. Lloyd's *Dynamic Idealism,* which appeared in 1898, is of considerable historical interest and remarkable for the way it mirrors the metamorphosis all these young idealists were undergoing in the nineties. It was the first book-length work to present their views and is just as valuable as Dewey's *Syllabus* to the student of this period in American philosophy. Dewey's *Syllabus,* it must be remembered, was just that, a syllabus, and so it was brief, dogmatic, and even oracular in tone. Lloyd's book, on the other hand, was certainly obscure, but at least comparatively detailed.

The title of Lloyd's book is very significant. The idealism Lloyd had in mind was dynamic, just as Dewey's was experimental. And Lloyd's idealism, like Dewey's, took as its first principle the idea that the self was not separated from the world. For Lloyd, the self is something always identified in activity with the world, or "in a commoner phrase," he says, "adjusted to the world." [8] This relation of adjustment between a self, or an organism, and the world is called a dynamic relation; it is not a formal relation, according to Lloyd.

Like Dewey in his book on Leibniz, Lloyd employs this honorific distinction between the favored dynamic relation and the scorned formal relation as a device with which to

[8] *Dynamic Idealism,* p. 14.

attack abstraction. First he argues that the fact of individuality makes abstraction or classification impossible. Since no two things are alike, you can never group things. But then he considers a possible question. Someone might say:

. . . while it is true that things are not to be classified in the ordinary way on account of their differences, may they not, do they not, have certain qualities through which a grouping of them is possible? Thus, red things form one class, regardless of their other characters; hard things another . . . and so on.[9]

To this Lloyd presents the following as an answer:

Yes, such a grouping of things as this is possible, but unfair to the things or to the so-called common quality. It neglects something in the things themselves. Different things do not even have common qualities. Qualities are not marks of things external to the things themselves. Most surely a red rose is not red as anything else is red. The redness of the rose is peculiar, because the rose itself is peculiar. No quality of anything can be independent of any of all its other qualities; and to assume an independence is to make the quality an altogether external mark, and then not a quality.[10]

This means that the relation which modern logicians call "class-membership" is an external relation and therefore falsifying in some sense. Because, obviously, if one individual is said to be red, then the property of being a red thing is assigned to it in a sense which permits the logician to say that some other individual has this same property, redness. Lloyd, on the contrary, would have us say, not simply "this table is red" and "that table is red," but "this table has the redness of this table" and "that table has the redness of that table." Expressed in this way, it becomes clear that the property you assign to *this* table when you say it is red is not the property you assign to *that* table when you say *it* is red. With the cogency of this argument we are not concerned. We merely observe how it permits Lloyd to argue

[9] *Ibid.*, p. 38.   [10] *Ibid.*, p. 38.

that unity by means of classification is a fake unity and that two things are never really united when they have some property in common. It follows that classes in the traditional sense disappear, class-membership becomes a useless, formal relation. This is exactly the effect of Dewey's contention in his book on Leibniz when he calls the unity achieved by calling two things members of the same aggregate "factitious." [11]

Having rejected the unity of classification, Lloyd presents another, the unity of organization. It is obvious, he says, that the sense in which two things are said to be united by being members of the same class is not the only sense of unity we employ. There is also the sense in which two things which are co-parts of a whole are said to be united. Some variant of this latter sense of unity is what Lloyd desperately tries to express in this book. His problem is similar to that of Morris, but he has the further problem of making his results seem consistent with the latest work in psychology and biology. The unity he introduces is the unity of composition, or organization. "The simple truth," he says, "is that composition involves an intrinsic unity of the component parts. In short, parts are more than mere

[11] LNE, p. 50. Lloyd's low regard for the unifying powers of class-abstraction is supported by arguments of a social and political nature. He says: "Many doctrines in science, some even of comparatively recent date, as well as many notions in every-day life and many institutions of society, have asserted or assumed the possibility of an identifying classification or of its counterpart, an isolating separation. The mediaeval doctrine of the genus, the doctrine of the immutability of species or persistence or disappearance of types, the Deductive Logic, the doctrine of inherited or acquired traits, the nativistic or intuitional theories of morals and religion, all the monarchical institutions of society, all systems of caste, are distinctly hostile to any real individuality, since they assume that individuals can be either herded under some common arbitrary head or excluded absolutely. All of them reduce the class to a mere composition of individuals united by no inner nature of their own, but by some external principle. All commit the sin of identifying unlikes or separating likes, or both. Natural enough has been the claim of monarchs to authority by divine right; and the reference of concepts or class-ideas to another world has been natural too, since the source of unity has been thought quite external to the things unified." *Dynamic Idealism*, pp. 39–40.

component parts; they are related parts, being related to each other with reference to the same end to which all are means." [12] Thus two parts of a chair are intrinsically united. For this reason Lloyd calls a chair, and in general any physical object, a *"system* of relations." And just as he considered an important objection to his attack on abstraction, he now considers a criticism of his view of physical objects. The imaginary objector says:

There is a wide difference between saying that things are relations and that things are related. Were they only relations, there could be no real things, no terms of relation, only pure formal relationship. A world of mere relations must be impossible, since there must be things, definite, real, substantial, among which formal relationship prevails. There must be cousins as well as cousinship, legs and arms as well as angles and other relationships that enter into the determination of a chair.[13]

That Lloyd should have converted all things into abstract entities like relations would have run counter to his earlier attack on classes. Therefore his first comment is that "relationship is other than the mere formal external condition that the objector here has in mind. Relationship is not formal but dynamic. It is, quite in and of itself, substantial. It cannot be both real and formal." [14] The net result of Lloyd's analysis is to eliminate all abstract entities in the conventional sense, and then to take the so-called "individuals," in the conventional usage, and convert them into relations or systems of relations in some new sense of the word "relation," according to which relations finally lose their abstractness and are identified with "activities." Every object, because it is relational, therefore *is* an activity; to use the later cliché, it *is* what it *does*. The world, because it, too, is a relational whole, is therefore active. It follows also that it is intelligible, because intelligibility means relationship.[15]

---

12 *Dynamic Idealism*, p. 40.   13 *Ibid.*, pp. 41–42.   14 *Ibid.*, p. 42.
15 *Ibid.*, pp. 42–52. Lloyd goes even further. He maintains that the world

The formal idealists, according to Lloyd, believed in the existence of ideas as forms, that is, in the existence of abstract entities. For them "the world of things and the world of ideas, or, more generally, matter and mind, must be two wholly distinct kingdoms of reality." [16] They are the pursuers of knowledge for knowledge's sake, the intellectual gymnasts, not the thinkers. For this reason, Lloyd says, militarism is the greatest living example of formal idealism.

The soldier is the very incarnation of Formal Idealism. His mind is not his own, for he is allowed only to know knowledge and to do deeds. His individual consciousness and his activity are two distinct things, and his body is medium not for any deeds of his own, but solely for those of God's kingdom, of Church and State, in which he trustingly lives, passive even through his greatest activity.[17]

In addition to this attack on drill, so closely associated with Dewey's theory of education at that time, there was also a conception of ideas as *forces,* not forms. The chapter on this in Lloyd's book is a good illustration of what William James meant when he said that Lloyd was "unassimilably obscure." Fortunately we are not concerned here with expounding Lloyd's philosophy in detail. But we are interested in his similarities to Dewey, and so it is important to find Lloyd saying the following:

A word . . . in popular discourse, expresses very well the true nature of an idea. The word is plan. Ideas are plans, and con-

---

is not only intelligible, but intelligent. He believes that all things live, and that to live is to think. Therefore he says: "The universe lives, and all life is intelligent. All life thinks. The universe thinks" (p. 53). Here we have the most extreme form of anti-dualism. Thought is everywhere. The world is an intelligent organism made up of intelligent organisms. An assault on dualism even stronger than Darwin's follows. For evolutionists at least believed that *some* things were inorganic. But not Lloyd; for him everything is organic (pp. 56–57). "Doubtless," he says, "this seems to approach very near to anthropomorphism, but anthropomorphism is not a reproach if one but see the man, to whom the world is likened, in his essential and world-wide, world-deep characteristics" (p. 59).

16 *Ibid.,* ch. vii.   17 *Ibid.,* p. 108.

sciousness is always a planning. . . . As plans, then, ideas are forces. What is planning but a process wherein manifold things, of which the planner is himself one, assume such an expression of their relations as will set activity free? [18]

The notion of ideas as plans appearing in a work as idealist in outlook as *Dynamic Idealism* is a perfect illustration of what is meant by saying that instrumentalism originates in idealism. Lloyd's work resembles that of the early Dewey even to the point of holding that biology confirmed his metaphysics. He says: "Biological speculation has reached this conclusion too, although in some quarters without any real appreciation of the identity of its thought with recent psychology." [19]

EVOLUTION AND CONFLICT

Although Dewey had formulated many views before he came into contact with evolutionary thought (just as Dewey claimed Leibniz had formulated his organicism before he read biology), when he came upon aspects of biological theory which seemed to confirm his views, he seized upon them. In the *Syllabus,* for instance, he tries to show how evolutionary thought supported his disbelief in the existence of immediate moral truths. We know that even in the *Psychology* Dewey denied that there was such a thing as immediate knowledge. He believed that those who held that there were immediately known truths must have postulated some special faculty for intuiting them. It followed that if he could disprove the existence of any such faculty, he would have refuted those who held there were immediate truths. In the *Syllabus* he calls the evolutionary theory to his support. The evolutionary position, he says, "leaves no room for the belief in any faculty of moral knowledge separate from the whole process of experience, and cuts the ground out from any store of information given directly and immediately." [20]

[18] *Ibid.,* p. 108.   [19] *Ibid.,* p. 84.   [20] *Syllabus,* p. 90.

This tendency to draw upon psychology, sociology, and biology to consolidate his gains was also expressed in 1894 in a piece called "Social Psychology." [21] It is a long review of a series of books, the most important of which are Lester Ward's *The Psychic Factors of Civilization* and Benjamin Kidd's *Social Evolution*. After criticizing the empiricist view of knowledge which Ward took over from Spencer, Dewey says a few words in praise of Ward's approach. He liked Ward's restatement of the evolutionary theory of the growth of intelligence. He summarizes it, in this way stating most succinctly the fundamental principle of his own thought for at least the next twenty years. According to the theory the key word in the discussion of the evolution of mind is "advantage." Advantage accrues when the animal increases his ability to satisfy his desires. Therefore he puts forth effort. But many desires cannot be satisfied by direct effort. "When a desire having a certain amount of active vigor at command meets obstacles, the result is that the animal is no longer simply checked." Because, although "external motion is arrested internal motility is increased." With the increase of "internal motility" the animal develops new points of attack, and thus by an indirect or flank movement finally reaches its goal. "This advantageous method would be selected and perpetuated until, finally, the power of mental exploration is developed." [22] Accordingly, Dewey says, intelligence is indirection—checking the natural, direct action and taking a circuitous course.

Ward's analysis, with all its virtues, is found by Dewey defective at one point, a point at which Kidd's is not. For Ward fails to see the positive evolutionary significance of conflict. "He seems to think," says Dewey, "that intellectual progress can now cut loose from the conditions under which it originated, namely preferential advantage in the struggle for existence." [23] Although Ward recognizes that man as a species attains intelligence as the end-point of a struggle, he seems to think that once he attains it, all the rest of his progress involves easy sailing. With this Dewey flatly disagrees. He says: "To me it appears as sure a psychological as biological principle that men go on thinking only because of practical friction or strain somewhere, that thinking is essentially the solution of tension." [24]

At this juncture Dewey has arrived at what may be called the specifically Deweyan view of "conflict." He begins with the Hegelian concept of conflict as we have noted. Philosophy, according to his 1884 paper on Kant, began with "contradictions." From them, by Hegelian syntheses, the solutions emerge. He then rides very easily on the wave of a newly gained naturalism into the Darwinian conflict doctrine. Man achieves intelligence in the course of a struggle for existence; again conflict. But now we come to the specifically Deweyan notion of conflict—the conflict, or tension, which characterizes human behavior in a problematic situation. The march is intricate and exciting—from Hegel to Darwin to Dewey. [25]

EVOLUTION AND ETHICS

Perhaps the most vigorous defense of evolutionary thought Dewey ever conducted was his criticism of Thomas

[23] *Ibid.*, p. 408.   [24] *Ibid.*, p. 408.

[25] This concern with conflict and struggle led to a detailed study of the Darwin and James-Lange theories of emotion, the results of which appeared in Dewey's "The Theory of Emotion" (*Psychological Review*, I, pp. 553–569, and II, pp. 13–32). The details of the analysis do not interest us. Suffice it to say that the paper is regarded as of great interest historically. The contemporary Russian psychologist, A. R. Luria, in his important work *The Nature of Human Conflicts*, New York, Liveright, 1932, says that Dewey, in "The Theory of Emotion," "was perhaps the first to show the close connection between emotion and human activity, advancing the hypothesis that emotion appears when human activity is obstructed" (p. 13). This obstruction of human activity leads to struggle or tension, the first step in Dewey's "five steps of reflective thought."

Huxley's Romanes lecture, "Evolution and Ethics." Huxley's lecture had been given in 1893, and Dewey's reply appeared in 1898, under the same title.

Huxley had shocked the intellectual world and confused his followers with this lecture. Up to that time a recognized leader of the Darwinists and all those who rejected any sharp break between man and nature, Huxley baffled his audience with what seemed like a complete surrender of his position. His lecture stressed the differences he thought existed between what he called the "cosmic" and the "ethical" processes. Dewey, apparently one of his startled followers, reports the reaction of his fellow-Darwinists and himself:

Those who recall the discussion following the lecture will remember that many felt as if they had received a blow knocking the breath out of their bodies. To some it appeared that Mr. Huxley had executed a sudden *volte-face* and had given up his belief in the unity of the evolutionary process, accepting the very dualistic idea of the separation between the animal and the human, against which he had previously directed so many hard blows.[26]

According to Huxley, the law of the cosmic process was struggle and strife, whereas the law of the ethical process was sympathy and coöperation. He said:

Social progress means the checking of the cosmic process at every step and the substitution for it of another, which may be called the ethical process. . . . Let us understand once for all that the ethical progress of society depends, not on imitating the cosmic process, still less in running away from it, but in combatting it.[27]

This conclusion is completely unacceptable to Dewey. He tries to undermine it by seizing upon certain concessions made by Huxley. He points to Huxley's statement that the ethical process, "strictly speaking, is part of the general cosmic process, just as the governor in a steam engine is

26 *Monist*, VIII, 323.
27 *Evolution and Ethics and Other Essays*, pp. 81–83.

part of the mechanism of the engine." [28] This concession is fastened upon by Dewey, for it permits him to get the ethical process within the cosmic process. In other words, to show that the desires for coöperation, sympathy, justice, etc. are themselves natural products which appear in the course of evolution. Surely then, Dewey maintains, they cannot be said to run counter to the entire cosmic process. Rather, Dewey thinks, Huxley is arguing that the *"part* of the cosmic process which is maintained in the conduct of men in society, is radically opposed both in its methods and aims to that *part* of the cosmic process which is exhibited in the stages of evolution prior to the appearance of socialized man upon the scene." [29] In the light of this analysis Dewey tries to reformulate the issue. He does this by taking an illustration of Huxley's, first drawing Huxley's conclusions and then presenting his own.

The illustration concerns the appearance of plants in a certain soil. They are adapted to that particular environment. Then man appears and he roots out the plants as harmful weeds; he introduces other plants to suit his own wants and aims. He also does many other things suited to his own needs, like building walls, fertilizing, varying conditions of moisture and sunlight. But finally, on Huxley's analysis, this artificial structure—the garden—is so opposed to the natural state of things that it deteriorates unless man keeps up his labors constantly.

Dewey tries to interpret the same facts differently. He admits that the gardener must struggle to keep his garden up. But, he claims, "we do not have here . . . a conflict of man as man with his entire natural environment. We have rather the modification by man of one part of the environment with reference to another part." [30] Dewey's argument is formally similar to the view he put forth in the *Syllabus*. There, impulses which do not harmonize with the main tendency of other impulses, are said to need transformation, reconstruction in the interest of some larger whole. On an individual scale this is the realization of the self in Dewey's (not Green's) sense. The self may be realized only if organized totally. For this reason a given impulse is neither good nor bad in itself. It may be evaluated only in the light of its contributing to the integration of behavior. The entire approach involves finding organic unities in terms of which the action of various parts is to be judged. In his 1898 paper on Huxley, Dewey turns this naturalized Greenianism to other problems. Certain products of the cosmic process conflict with others. In this case the weeds conflict with man's desire to have a beautiful garden. But now that man has appeared as a high-point in the cosmic process, there is a larger whole to be considered. Things will be said to be "fit" in this cosmic process only in so far as they satisfy the needs of socialized man. By virtue of its late appearance, the behavior of man forms the widest unity and determines which things are cosmically fit. Therefore Dewey says:

The conditions with respect to which the term "fit" must *now* be used include the existing social structure with all the habits, demands, and ideals which are found in it. If so, we have reason to conclude that the "fittest" with respect to the whole of the conditions is the best; that indeed, the only standard we have of the best is the discovery of that which maintains these conditions in their integrity. The unfit is practically the anti-social.[31]

What Dewey inferred from Huxley's contention was the belief that there is constant struggle between an organ adjusted to a past state and functions required by present conditions. The "fittest," who are tigers and apes, are the fittest of former days, whose struggle techniques become antiquated when socialized man appears. Therefore there is tension between the rapacious who got that way struggling to exist and man, whose adjustment involves a different kind

[31] *Ibid.,* p. 326.

of behavior. This tension demands solution. Old organs must be trained to adapt to new circumstances. Habits must be changed to meet new difficulties. An organic unity must be reinstated. And this organic unity is the unity of the cosmic process, whose ideal is the social happiness of man.

There was also a deeper significance to this paper on evolution and ethics. It subtly combines Dewey's idealist view of the norm as not coming *ab extra* with evolutionary theory. And this, I think, was repeated in Dewey's first essay in the *Studies in Logical Theory*.

CHAPTER NINE

EVOLUTION AND ARITHMETIC

The evolutionary method of seeking out origins was first applied by Dewey on a large scale in *The Psychology of Number,* written with J. A. McLellan in 1895. The application of the method in the sphere of number is of considerable interest, because it is Dewey's first attempt to deal with a formal concept. There is an obvious sense in which the notion of number is the mathematician's concern. If one says "5 is a number" the analysis of the meaning of this statement is no less the concern of the mathematician than is the analysis of the meaning of the statement "2 is the only even prime number." This was taken seriously by Frege, who pursued the analysis of the concept of number. The result of his analysis was that number could be defined in terms of the concepts of mathematical logic so that any statement involving the word "number" could be eliminated in favor of statements involving expressions like "class," "similar," "is a member of," etc., and for any statement in which particular numerals appeared, one could formulate an equivalent statement in which these numerals were supplanted by logical expressions. Finally, if one set up a system of logic, all the theorems of arithmetic could be deduced from this system of logic.

Simply because the Frege approach afforded an analysis of the concept of number, one could not reject all other theories that discussed number. Some of them, like that suggested by the title of Dewey's book, could discuss the *psychology* of number and never conflict with Frege's analysis. They would concern different things. For instance, one of the problems Dewey wished to discuss in this book concerned "the interest, the demand which gives rise to the psychical activity by which objects are taken as numbered." [1] In another place, after pointing out that the sense of number has a historical, evolutionary development and that it arises in the race and in the individual, he says: "The psychological (and the pedagogical) problem is: Under what circumstances, in response to what stimuli or needs, in what psychical context, does this sense arise?" [2] Dewey makes clear that he wishes to find out a psychological-historical fact— the circumstance under which the human activity of assigning number arises. Compare this with Russell's question, which is simply "What is a number?" [3]

The difference between the two approaches has been emphasized for purposes of the discussion to follow. This does not mean that Dewey would have accepted the distinction I have been making or even that he accepts it today. It is true that he comes close to accepting it in a controversy with H. B. Fine, the mathematician. Moreover, we cannot forget his definition of "triangle" in 1891, where he insisted that the correct answer to the question "What is a triangle?" could only be determined by finding out how the triangle came to be. Obviously, if this kind of genetic approach were to have continued only four short years, it would have committed Dewey to saying that the above historical questions were really equivalent to the question "What is a number?" It would follow, of course, that our sharp distinction between the Frege-Russell question and the Dewey question would have to dissolve on Dewey's view. And, in fact, this is what happens at many places in the *Psychology of Num-*

[1] *Psychology of Number,* p. 22.
[2] *Psychological Review,* III, 327 (a book review).
[3] *Introduction to Mathematical Philosophy,* New York, Macmillan, 1919. p. 11.

ber. Dewey surreptitiously shifts from a statement about the history and origin of number to a statement about the nature of number. It would be valuable to study these passages in Dewey without first going into a general discussion of the relation between origin and nature, and the genetic fallacy, etc., although these are probably involved.

"Number is to be traced to measurement, and measurement back to adjustment of activity." [4] This is the theme of the book, and its explanation is a long evolutionary statement. Man, Dewey says, lived in a world in which the supply of necessary things was limited. This meant that he had to put forth effort. The struggle to get his goods made him interested in the limits of his supply. Thus the idea of quantity arose, as a means of assigning limits to stock or future stock. In the course of his efforts to gather his goods he spent a considerable amount of energy. It therefore became necessary to economize energy—to dispose of it so as to accomplish the best possible results. And since "we carry out our plans most successfully . . . when we accurately adjust our energies to the thing required," [5] we begin to measure. If there were no problem of adjusting relations between means and ends, Dewey maintains, the necessity for measurement would not exist, and there would be no such thing as number. But, since the check to our activity and the limits of our supply defer the satisfaction of our needs, the end becomes remote and complex, "and in using adequate means, distance in space, remoteness in time, quantity of some sort has to be taken into account, and this means accurate measurement." [6] The end must be exactly balanced by the means. "Not too much, not too little" energy should be devoted to the solution of any problem.

. . . it is this necessity of exact balance or equivalency which transforms the vague quantitative ideas of smaller and greater, heavy and light, and so on, into the definite quantitative ideas of

⁴ *Psychology of Number,* p. 53.   ⁵ *Ibid.,* p. 37.   ⁶ *Ibid.,* p. 37.

just so distant, just so long, so heavy, so elastic, etc. This demands the introduction of the idea of *number*. Number is the definite measurement, the definite valuation of a quantity falling within a given limit.[7]

H. B. Fine reviewed *The Psychology of Number*. His conclusion was that although the book advocated good methods of teaching arithmetic, it made a false analysis of the number concept.[8] And his chief criticism of the analysis of the number is stated as follows:

The conviction of [the] authors that the difficulties which children have with arithmetic are due to the neglect of teachers to lay sufficient stress on the metrical function of number has carried them to the extreme of maintaining that number is essentially metrical in its nature and origin.[9]

The claim that number is metrical in *origin* was one thing; the claim that it was metrical in *nature* was another. Fine disagreed with both, but surely more strongly with the latter.[10] His major concern was to show, in opposition to Dewey and McLellan, that counting is not identical with measuring. You measure the length of something, for instance, by taking a standard rule and applying it. But you do not count a bunch of berries by taking a standard berry and applying it repeatedly. That Dewey maintained the latter position in some form is obvious in the following passage:

. . . we are accustomed to distinguish counting (i. e., numeration, numbering) from measuring. It is usually said that we count objects, particular things or qualities to see how *many* of them there are, while we measure a particular object or quality

---

[7] *Ibid.,* p. 42. [8] *Science,* N.S., III (1896), 134. [9] *Ibid.,* p. 134.

[10] Fine, who was professor of mathematics at Princeton, was very advanced in his interest in the foundations of mathematics. He collaborated with Charles Peirce on the article entitled "Multitude" in Baldwin's *Dictionary of Philosophy and Psychology,* and his *College Algebra* contains a very good introduction to number theory. In his little book *The Number System of Algebra* he indicates full knowledge of the work of Weierstrass and George Cantor. His knowledge of the latter's work is reflected in his comments on set theory and in his Cantorian treatment of the irrationals.

to see how *much* of it there is. We count chairs, beds, splints, feet, eyes, children, stamens, etc., simply to get their sum total, the *how many;* we measure distance, weight, bulk, price, cost, etc., to see *how much* there is. Some writers say that these "two kinds of quantity," which they call quantity of magnitude (how much) and quantity of multitude (how many), are entirely distinct. Nevertheless, all counting is measuring, and all measuring is counting. When we count up the number of particular books in a library we *measure* the library—find out how much it amounts to as a library; when we count the days of the year, we measure the time value of the year; when we count children in a class, we measure the class as a whole—it is a large or a small class, etc. When we count stamens or pistils we measure the flower. In short, when we count we measure.[11]

To say, as Dewey does, that all counting is measuring and all measuring is counting is to say that measuring is the same as counting. But Fine argues that this is not true. For by measuring he meant finding out how much, that is, magnitude. When you perform certain operations on a rod and conclude that the rod is five feet long, you measure the rod. Thus one says: "If you apply a footrule to rod *a,* then rod *a* is five feet long if and only if you can make five applications of this rule on rod *a.*" I offer this only as a possible analysis and as an illustration. What I wish to emphasize is that whatever the precise way of formulating the statement which defines what it means for a particular object to be five feet long, we may be sure that the formulation will contain nonarithmetical and nonlogical constants in addition to the name of the object measured. Thus in the above statement the word "footrule" appears as well as the phrase "apply a footrule." These terms are neither of logic, nor of arithmetic, nor definable by means of only logical or arithmetical terms. They are physical constants. Any definition of a metrical concept would make use of such terms, because the *definiens* would always contain the name of a metrical standard.

11 *Psychology of Number,* pp. 47–48.

Fine maintained that the problem is entirely different in the case of counting. His point is expressed most accurately in terms of Frege's analysis. If I count a group of horses and conclude that there are two horses, my statement can be shown equivalent to a statement in which the only nonlogical, nonarithmetical term that turns up is the name of the particular group of horses I am counting. If I had said "The number of horses running in the Kentucky Derby in 1941 is 2," I could translate this into a statement in which only terms of logic and the expression "The class of horses running in the Kentucky Derby in 1941" would appear. This is a direct consequence of Frege's analysis.[12] It is also what is meant when one says that number is a logical concept, not a metrical concept, and it makes precise Fine's contention that "no one ever did or ever will count a group of horses, for instance, by first conceiving of an artificial unit horse and then matching it with each actual horse in turn—which 'measuring' the group of horses must mean if it means anything." [13]

Dewey replied to Fine's review of his book in a letter. In his reply he does not meet Fine directly, nevertheless he says some important things from the point of view of his later development. The comments are interesting because of their connection with some of his views on formal logic, interesting enough to reproduce at length. Dewey says, as he really avoids Fine's fundamental criticism,

The whole point here is under what circumstances does one, not a mathematician or for mathematical purposes, count a group of horses. The answer is something of the following sort, it seems to me: One counts when one wishes to find out how many horses he has caught in a day's hunt, whether the same number has been driven back at night that were taken out in the morning; how much money is to be got in selling them, it having been

12 See Tarski, *op. cit.*, sections 20, 26, 33 for an elementary account of the reduction of number to logical constants.
13 *Science*, N.S., III, 135.

settled that each horse is to fetch the same sum, etc., etc.; how one ranks as a chieftain, or a soldier, compared with others, etc., etc. In other words, one not having arrived at the *abstract* interest of the mathematician (and certainly the child to be educated has not) counts only *when* there is some value to be ascertained, and counts *by* setting off something which, for present purposes is a sample unit of value, e. g., a horse, then equating the total value to the number of such units.[14]

Throughout his letter Dewey insists that he is not talking within the domain of mathematics or its foundations, but rather that he is making an anthropological judgment concerning the origin of concepts which at a later date in evolution become the mathematician's concern, in short that his book is concerned with the conceptual ancestor of number. He says:

The trained mathematician as such is, of necessity, interested in the further use of certain finished psychical products. As a mathematician any reference to the preliminary development of these products can only disturb or divert him. But the problem for the pupil *is how to get the standpoint of the mathematician;* not how to use certain tools but how to make them; not how to carry further the manipulation of certain data, but how to get meaning into the data. This is ultimately a psychological question, not a mathematical one, although it has to be translated over into mathematical terms and processes; and none is so well fitted to do it as the mathematician, provided only he will project himself far enough backward in the scale of development to realize the problem. The point does not conclude with primary instruction. Our text-books of algebra and high analysis are almost entirely written from the standpoint of an elegant and logical exposition of the matter as it stands to the trained mathematician. They are very nice for one who doesn't need them any longer. The first books written from the standpoint of one who is still coming to consciousness of the meaning of his concepts will, perhaps, seem foolishness to the trained mathematician, but they will mark the dawn of a new day to the average student. I venture the statement that (putting aside the few with the inborn mathematical instinct) higher and secondary

14 *Science*, N.S. III, 287.

mathematics is to the majority of students a practical riddle with no definite *intellectual* content in itself. What meaning it possesses it has got by way of attained practical facility in solving problems; or through its applications to other sciences or to engineering. It will hardly be denied that the educational value of mathematics is not realized until its concepts and methods have a definite intellectual meaning and content of their own. Can this be secured, save as the methods of instruction follow the evolution of the process out of its cruder psychical forms to the more finished? [15]

This reply leaves Dewey's position on number at that time more unclear than ever. For if Fine's critique be formulated in terms of Frege's analysis, as I have formulated it above, it is clear that Dewey was not offering a logistic account of number. There remains the possibility that he was groping toward an analysis of number according to which it cannot be defined solely in terms of logical constants. But a reading of Dewey's letter suggests that he was not interested in making a last-ditch stand for his view of number as a magnitude similar to weight, but rather that he was interested only in maintaining that the theory of number he was presenting adequately described the way children used numbers. However, apart from any specific analysis of number the book presents, it has great historical value. For it puts forth a distinction between the study of formal concepts as formal and a study of the psychology of formal concepts. The *Psychology of Number* looks backward to Dewey's antagonism to formalism and forward to his instrumental logic. His letter in answer to Fine suggests that he is beginning to accept the formal approach as adequate in its own sphere, but that he is not interested in it. He wishes to point out that there are other serious problems to be investigated, problems concerning the biology, sociology, and psychology of formal thought.

[15] *Science*, N.S. III, p. 288.

CHAPTER TEN

LOTZE AND INSTRUMENTAL LOGIC

Dewey has said that his earliest writings were relatively clear, that his youthful prose was direct and uninvolved. Presumably his subservience to an already existing mode of thought, his attachment to the words of his masters, made it easy for him to talk a language understood by many, if not by all. It was only later, he thinks, when he began to try to create new ideas, to say things he thought had not been said before, that he began to be troubled about his prose style, about his capacity to communicate his thoughts to others. If this is true, and there is considerable evidence for it, one might easily say that the four essays which Dewey published in the *Studies in Logical Theory* (1903) were the climactic works of his career. They are very difficult reading, partly no doubt because they criticize views with which readers of today are not familiar. The important point, however, is that they are not the expression of views held by any school of thought existing in 1903; they represent, as William James said, a *"new* school of thought." They stand as the first detailed expression of Dewey's new ideas, the first long reports on the investigations he and Lloyd and Mead had been at for twelve years.

LOTZE, IDEALISM, AND DEWEY

The *Studies in Logical Theory* were the fruits of Dewey's work on logic during the nineties. His silence on logical matters was no proof that he was not working on problems which he considered logical. He had been teaching courses in logic, in connection with which he had been studying the texts of Mill, Lotze, Bosanquet, and Bradley. Lotze in particular engaged Dewey's attention. Readers of the essays which Dewey contributed to the *Studies* know of their concern with Lotze. It is sometimes said (no doubt because little of Dewey's earliest work is read today) that Dewey had been a Lotzean and that the *Studies* were the first statements of his revolt against Lotze. But this is not true, and something should be said about the relation between Dewey's ideas before the *Studies*, his position in the *Studies*, and Lotze's views on thought.

A good way to get at this is to examine Henry Jones' *Critical Account of the Philosophy of Lotze*, published in 1895. It is an extremely useful picture of the relation between Lotze and English idealist logic. Moreover, it is a book with which Dewey was very familiar and upon which he drew considerably. It is also important for our purposes because Jones subscribed, in general, to the position which Dewey had taken during his idealist period. In a rough way, Jones' book offers us a means of telling to what extent Lotze was an idealist (in the eyes of an idealist); to what extent Dewey's opinion of Lotze coincided with Jones' (and thereby a means of telling to what extent Dewey's criticism derived from idealism); and finally, a means of telling to what extent Dewey's criticisms of Lotze were *not* the same as idealist criticisms of him (and thereby a means of telling, by comparison, what was original in Dewey's thought at that time).

Jones points out in his Preface that Lotze opposed Hegel and his followers for believing that thought and reality are identical.[1] Lotze believed that thought did not constitute reality, but rather that it represented it. Jones held that if

[1] Page vii.

Lotze's view of thought were true, the idealistic view would be "entirely broken," because then "Thought, instead of being the substance of things seen, and the principle whi⸗ lives and moves in all objects of intelligence, is only a part . . . of man's mental equipment."[2] "But," Jones adds,

Lotze's investigation of thought has had other and more valuable consequences. It has led modern writers to investigate the nature of thought for themselves, with the result that, particularly in this country, there has been a remarkable development of logical theory along Lotze's lines. I refer more specially to the logical works of Mr. Bradley and Mr. Bosanquet, to whom I express with great pleasure deep obligations. This development of Lotze's position seems to me to issue in its refutation; and there are indications that the main contribution of Lotze to philosophic thought, the only ultimate contribution, consists in deepening that idealism which he sought to overthrow.[3]

Bradley and Bosanquet, then, were influenced by Lotze and stimulated by him to investigate the questions he had investigated, but according to Jones they concluded by proving the very thing Lotze had wanted to refute.

It has been my endeavor in this volume [Jones says] to justify this conclusion in detail. That is to say, I have tried to lay bare the movement of Lotze's exposition, so as to show not only that it refutes itself, but that it indicates in a new way the necessity for an idealistic construction of experience. For if Lotze had been faithful to the view of thought which he sets forth and which he attributes to Idealists, he would have found it incapable of performing that poor remnant of its functions which he allows it to retain. In order to get his formal thought to produce any results he is constrained to find each of its products one by one in its material. Hence, what he exposes to our view is a kind of pseudo-dialectic by which, on the failure of one form of abstract thought after another, he has recourse to its content. Each fresh appeal to content gives to formal thought a fresh start, and the possibility of thinking at all is thus, by implication, shown to lie in its material. The very helplessness of formal thought at once indicates that *such* thought is a logical fiction

---

[2] *Ibid.*, p. xi. [3] *Ibid.*, pp. xii–xiii.

and bears witness to the ideality of its content. On his own showing the material dominates thought and expresses *itself* in thought. In this way, therefore, Lotze leads us from a formal to a constitutive view of thought. That is to say, in expounding the conditions of its activity, he yields *a tergo*, and as an unwilling witness, an idealistic conception of the world.[4]

It will not be necessary to quote any more from Jones' book in order to show how close his attack on Lotze is to Dewey's. Nor will readers of the *Studies* fail to recall how Dewey allies himself with and dissociates himself from the neo-Hegelian criticism of Lotze. Dewey considered the question in his second study. He says: "The notion that value or significance as distinct from mere existentiality is the product of thought or reason, and that the source of Lotze's contradiction lies in the effort to find *any* situation prior or antecedent to thought, is a familiar one." [5] He adds that it is even possible that some of his readers may have interpreted his criticisms of Lotze in this way. "This position [the so-called neo-Hegelian one] and that taken in this chapter do agree in certain general regards," Dewey says, after pointing out his indebtedness to Jones in a footnote on p. 43.

They are at one in the denial of the factuality and the possibility of developing fruitful reflection out of antecedent bare existence or mere events. They unite in denying that there is or can be anything such as mere existence—phenomenon unqualified as respects meaning, whether such phenomenon be psychic or cosmic. They agree that reflective thought grows organically out of experience which is already organized, and that it functions within such an organism.[6]

Here, of course, we find Dewey reflecting the organicism of his idealist days. It remains for him to say in what way he no longer accepts idealist organicism. His view and the idealist view, he says,

[4] *Ibid.*, pp. xiii–xiv.   [5] *Studies in Logical Theory*, p. 43.
[6] *Ibid.*, pp. 43–44.

part company when a fundamental question is raised: Is all organized meaning the work of thought? Does it therefore follow that the organization out of which reflective thought grows is the work of thought of some other type—of Pure Thought, Creative or Constitutive Thought, Intuitive Reason, etc.? I shall indicate briefly reasons for divergence at this point.[7]

In giving reasons for diverging from idealism Dewey relies on two considerations. First of all, he says, "the more one insists that the antecedent situation is constituted by thought, the more one has to wonder why another type of thought is required; what need arouses it, and how it is possible for it to improve upon the work of previous constitutive thought."[8] He also asks how it happens that the absolute constitutive thought does such a poor and bungling job that it requires a finite discursive activity to patch up its products. In answer to this Dewey says the idealist must say that the Absolute Reason works under "limiting conditions of finitude, of a sensitive and temporal organism."[9] But then Dewey raises a second objection: "How can thought relate itself to the fragmentary sensations, impressions, feelings, which, in their contrast with and disparity from the workings of constitutive thought, mark it off from the latter . . ." Dewey concludes that the absolute rationalist will be thrown into the problem with which Lotze began: "we have the same insoluble question of the reference of thought-activity to a wholly indeterminate, unrationalized, independent, prior existence."[10]

Dewey is willing to admit only that certain elements of the antecedent situation are stable and that in this sense thinking does not begin with mere sensation. Parts of the problematic situation are determinate. Meaning, therefore, is present before any particular inquiry is begun. Only when the problem is taken out of its context in actual thought-situations does a dichotomy arise between a fixed set of bare sensations and a foreign activity which is performed

7 *Ibid.*, p. 44.   8 *Ibid.*, p. 44.   9 *Ibid.*, p. 45.   10 *Ibid.*, p. 45

on them. If the logician examines actual thinking, he will find that sensation, perception, judgment, and inference are all concepts which refer to phases of the doubt-inquiry process. As phases of a total process, they are linked and pass into each other. Once this is recognized, one cannot set up two orders—impressions and thoughts—in a way which makes it impossible to see how perception and theory ever unite in the solution of specific problems.

The quotations from Jones and Dewey illustrate the general relation which existed between Jones, the representative of British idealism, Lotze, and the Dewey of the *Studies*. Jones and Dewey are in coalition against Lotze, but not in a coalition which presupposes absolute unity of opinion. Although Dewey cites the same defects in Lotze that the idealists criticize, he refuses to go on to postulate a constitutive thought. He does not think, as Jones does, that the critique which the latter levels against Lotze necessarily involves an acceptance of any kind of thought but that which human beings carry on every day of their lives. The *Studies*, when examined in the light of this situation, take on added interest. Because every argument which Dewey adduces for his refusal to go the whole way with the idealists may be regarded as a part of the original philosophy he was trying to build. Moreover, every argument against Lotze which can be found in Jones, may be labeled, with a fair amount of assurance, as the idealist element in Dewey's thought.

THE GENERAL PROBLEM OF LOGICAL THEORY

We have already seen that Dewey's opposition to Lotze springs from a disagreement about what the problem of logical theory is. The first study in the *Studies* is a statement of the positive convictions which motivate Dewey's entire contribution to the volume. It is, in effect, a statement of Dewey's general logical views at the time. The remaining

studies by Dewey are only applications of this machinery
to the text of Lotze. And although the first study is also a
polemic against Lotze, it revolves around more general
topics, so that it may be discussed without first presenting
a detailed account of Lotze's views.

The keynote of Dewey's first study is what he calls "the
principle of continuity." The acceptance of this principle,
which is never explicitly formulated in the *Studies*, is what
connects almost every specific philosophic contention in
the first essay. Even if it be regarded as the vague declaration
that there are no sharp breaks in human experience, it can
be seen to unite the following theses of the first study.

THOUGHT IS DERIVATIVE AND SECONDARY

This is the first contention of the essay. Thought is said
to come after something, out of something, and for the
sake of something.[11] It is because thought is a human activity
which precedes and follows other kinds of human activity
that we say thought is *continuous* with these other types of
activity. This view is directed against those who set up
thought as a nonhuman activity, radically different from
other activities like (to use Dewey's illustrations) conversa-
tion with a friend, drawing a plan for a house, walking,
eating dinner, purchasing a suit of clothes.[12] The continuity,
we may infer from Dewey's language in the first study, is
expressed simply by saying that all these activities are performed by human beings. If this seemed too trivial to af-
firm, Dewey would have pointed to all those philosophers
who believed in the existence of constitutive thought.

THE OPPOSITION TO LOTZE'S "PURE LOGIC"

Lotze had distinguished between two kinds of logic—
pure and applied. The first part of his *Logic,* he said, would
treat "pure or formal logic," which is "devoted to thought

11 *Ibid.*, p. 1.   12 *Ibid.*, pp. 2–3.

in general and those universal forms and principles of thought which hold good everywhere, both in judging of reality and in weighing possibility, irrespective of any difference in objects." [13]

Pure logic [Lotze says] itself will show and explain that the forms of concept, judgment, and syllogism are to be considered primarily as *ideal* forms, which give to the matter of our ideas, if we succeed in arranging it under them, its true logical setting. But the different peculiarities of different objects offer resistance to this arrangement; it is not clear of itself what sum of matter has a claim to form a determinate concept and be opposed to another, or which predicate belongs universally to which subject, or how the universal law for the arrangement of a manifold material is to be discovered. Applied logic is concerned with those methods of investigation which obviate these defects. It considers hindrances and the devices by which they may be overcome; and it must therefore sacrifice the love of systematization to considerations of utility and select what the experience of science has so far shown to be important and fruitful.[14]

The third investigation which is carried on in Lotze's *Logic,* but which is not labeled as some *kind* of logic, is called "methodology." It deals with the "question how far the most complete structure of thought . . . can claim to be an adequate account of that which we seem compelled to assume as the object and occasion of our ideas." [15]

Dewey's objections to this parceling out of the logician's tasks are registered in the first study. He accuses Lotze of postulating a "thought-in-itself," presumably that thing which Lotze planned to study in his "pure" logic. Dewey is shocked to find that according to Lotze's view, applied logic, the investigation of actual thinking, had to be carried on only to deal with the hindrances to pure thinking. And finally, he expresses his opposition to any view which assumes the solvability of the problem: "How do the specifica-

[13] Lotze, *Logic*, 2d ed., I, 10–11.
[14] *Ibid.*, p. 11.   [15] *Ibid.*, p. 12.

tions of thought as such hold good of reality as such?" [16]
In this way he dismisses two parts of Lotze's enterprise as
meaningless and construes one, applied logic, as the only
one worth pursuing—provided it is not interpreted in the
way Lotze interprets it.

Instead of formulating the problems of logic in the
manner of Lotze, Dewey, by using his principle of continuity, dispenses with pure logic as a discipline. He believes
that the notion of pure logic is based on the notion of pure
thought, which, in turn, springs from dualistic premises to
which Lotze is committed. These are not attacked in detail
in the first study, but Dewey does state a contrasting view
of the problems of logical theory. The point stressed is that
the logician, like any other student of human activity, must
make an empirical inquiry into thought. In this way the
thesis that thought is continuous with other human activities leads to the thesis that pure logic, when it pretends to
study "pure thought," is inadequate. The question as to
whether formal logic is a worth-while discipline is hardly
touched. What Dewey is anxious to deny is that there is
any study which is pure and at the same time about thinking. Whether the kind of work which the mathematical
logicians of the nineteenth century carried on also met with
Dewey's disapproval is not clear in the *Studies*. When he
attacks pure logic there, he attacks the view that we can find
out something about thought by an a priori method. In
effect, he thinks that logic, as he construes it, is an empirical
science.

THE IDENTIFICATION OF LOGIC AND "THE NATURAL HISTORY OF THOUGHT"

There were some problems which Lotze explicitly eliminated from logic. He said:

[16] *Studies in Logical Theory*, p. 6.

What particular tone of mind is required for successful thinking, how the attention is to be kept up, distraction avoided, tor-
pidity stimulated, precipitation checked, all these are questions
which no more belong to the field of logic than do enquiries
about the origin of our sense-impressions and the conditions
under which consciousness in general and conscious activity are
possible. We may presuppose the existence of all these things,
of perceptions, ideas, and their connexion according to the laws
of a psychical mechanism, but logic only begins with the conviction that the matter cannot end here; the conviction, that
between the combinations of ideas, however they may have originated, there is a difference of truth and untruth, and that
there are forms which these combinations *ought* to answer and
laws which they *ought* to obey. It is true that we may attempt
a psychological investigation to explain the origin of this authoritative consciousness itself; but the only standard by which
the correctness of our results could be measured would be one
set up by the very consciousness to be investigated. The first
thing, then, that has to be ascertained is, *what* the contents of
this authoritative conviction are; the history of its growth can
only have a secondary place, and even then must conform to the
requirements of its own imposing.[17]

It is this contention of Lotze, especially the second clause
in the last sentence, against which Dewey argues strenuously. It is this approach which Dewey opposes when he
argues for a genetic approach. His attacks in the *Studies* are
dispersed, yet they indicate in what way he found himself
opposing a nongenetic approach in logic.

Dewey wished to argue, in opposition to Lotze, that the
logician could formulate the criteria of good thinking only
by examining thinking. He refused to distinguish the task
of describing thought as something with which the psychologist deals, from the task of evaluating it as something with
which the logician is supposed to struggle. Both jobs, he
thought, were intimately related, and those who sharply
separated them he regarded as dualists. Neither job, he

[17] Lotze, *op. cit.,* p. 10.

thought, was one for "pure" logic, where that is supposed to study pure thought. The logician, in his opinion, was supposed to "follow the natural history of thinking as a life process having its own generating antecedents and stimuli, its own states and career, and its own specific objective and limit." [18] "This point of view," he says, "makes it possible for logical theory to come to terms with psychology." Psychology is not regarded as the science of genesis, set over against logic, the science of validity. Therefore he refuses to believe that the logician "is concerned, not with genesis, but with value, not with a historic cycle, but with absolute distinctions and relations." [19]

If we ask in what sense the logician engages in a genetic study, we find a rough answer in Dewey's first study. First of all, if the thinking process is a cycle—as Dewey claimed it is—then the logician, as the recorder of a cycle, is engaged in a study of development. In this respect he studies "the natural history of thought." The further question is: In what sense is the logician who formulates the conditions for valid thinking, also engaged in a genetic study? The answer is not detailed. In a sense it raises a question with which Dewey never dealt at length before his *Logic* appeared. There are, however, some arguments in its favor which appear in the *Studies*.

The major argument is based on what Dewey thought were the results of evolutionary biology. Dewey exclaimed at one point: "It is astonishing that in the face of the advance of evolutionary method in natural science, any logician can persist in the assertion of a rigid difference between the problem of origin and nature; between genesis and analysis; between history and validity." [20] Natural history, according to the Darwinian view, as Dewey construed the Darwinian view, treated "every distinct organ, structure,

---

[18] *Studies*, p. 13.   [19] *Ibid.*, p. 14.   [20] *Ibid.*, p. 14.

or formation, every grouping of cells or elements . . . as an instrument of adjustment or adaptation to a particular environing situation." [21] From this Dewey inferred that thought was an instrument of adjustment to an environing situation. If, now, we judge an activity good according to the degree to which it achieves its end—adjustment—then it follows that thinking is good or valid to the extent to which it achieves adjustment.

The form of the argument may be stated in a general way. The argument begins with the psychological or biological observation that certain activities have adjustment as their "natural goal." This is a judgment in natural history; it describes a fact. That thought is such an activity is also established empirically. Then the method involves taking adjustment as the basis for constructing a criterion of validity. It takes that which it finds to be the natural goal of a certain kind of activity and says that all instances of that kind of activity are good only if they attain this goal. The notion of a natural goal is not very clear, but clear enough to permit one to see that it is not something which every instance of the kind of activity under consideration attains. Thus thinking may have as its goal the clearing up of a conflicting situation, but this does not mean that all instances of thinking do in fact resolve the problems they start with. The fact that something is the natural goal of a certain kind of activity is established in a way which is not discussed by Dewey; it is taken for granted as demonstrated in evolutionary biology. But assuming that the idea of a natural goal can be made clear, it becomes easier to understand how the attainment of this goal is set up as a standard of success. Dewey summarizes his point as follows: "The historical point of view describes the sequence; the normative follows the sequence to its conclusion, and then turns back and

21 *Ibid.*, p. 15.

judges each historical step by viewing it in reference to its own outcome." [22]

This view of logic as the natural history of thought guides Dewey's entire discussion of concepts which he considered logical. If thought is a doubt-inquiry process, then all the distinctions which the logician makes are supposed to correspond to certain phases in the development of thought. In particular, the question of thought and its subject matter is discussed in this way. The antecedent of thought is taken to be a conflicting situation; the data of thought are things which emerge from this situation in the early stages of inquiry; the object of thought corresponds to a later period in the development of a given inquiry. Dewey feels that it would be impossible to define these notions without making reference to the procedure of inquiry. Early in his second study Dewey tells the reader that the last three studies will be concerned with "three quite distinct forms" assumed by the subject matter of thought in the development of thought. "I shall attempt to show that we must consider subject-matter from the standpoint, first of the *antecedents* or conditions that evoke thought; second, of the *datum* or *immediate material* presented to thought; and, third, of the proper content of thought." About the distinction Dewey says something which presents the whole method of the *Studies:*

It goes without saying that these are to be discriminated as stages of a life-process in the natural history of experience, not as ready-made or ontological; it is contended that, save as they are differentiated in connection with well-defined historical stages, they are either lumped off as equivalents, or else treated as absolute divisions—or as each by turns, according to the exigencies of the argument. [23]

The criticism which Dewey levels against Lotze involves a detailed application of this method. The concrete results

---

[22] *Ibid.,* p. 16.   [23] *Ibid.,* p. 24.

of this critique of Lotze become commonplace in the later writings of Dewey.

In summary, it may be said that the *Studies* and their thesis of logic as the natural history of thought, their principle of continuity, their opposition to constitutive thought, make up the first lengthy statement of the position which was later to become instrumentalism. A program was implicit in them, and in Dewey's paper "Some Stages of Logical Thought." [24] This paper was the first in which he criticized transcendental logic. The latter, he said, claims,

by an analysis of science and experience, to justify the conclusion that the universe itself is a construction of thought, giving evidence throughout of the pervasive and constitutive action of reason, and holds, consequently, that our logical processes are simply the reading off or coming to consciousness of the inherently rational structure already possessed by the universe in virtue of the presence within it of this pervasive and constitutive action of thought.[25]

Dewey could no longer accept any constitutive thought, for he believed at the time that thinking is a "doubt-inquiry process." It should be clear that the conception of thought and knowledge which Dewey was surrendering at the turn of the century, was the very conception he had put forth earlier, in his *Psychology*. There, he wholeheartedly subscribed to the view that knowledge-getting was a reading off of meanings previously instituted by an absolute intelligence. A comparison of Dewey's views of knowledge in the *Psychology* and in the *Studies*, would show the vivid contrasts and extremes in Dewey's development.

The break with idealism on the nature of thought, as expressed at that time, marked the closing of Dewey's attachment to idealist philosophy. For ten years he had been trying to untie difficult transcendental knots. In 1900 he

24 *Philosophical Review*, IX (1900), 465–489; reprinted in *Essays in Experimental Logic* (1916), pp. 183–219.
25 *Essays in Experimental Logic*, p. 217.

gave up the job and cut the slender strings that tied him to Morris, Green, and Caird. By 1903 he was an ex-idealist in ethics, psychology, and logic.

All other traditional avenues of logical thought were closed. Aristotelian logic was anathema to him. So was the logic of Mill and his followers. Mathematical logic was something of which he knew almost nothing and about which he probably cared less. The only way out was to construct his own theory of thought, beginning with his firm belief that thought is a doubt-inquiry process. Dewey faced the task of building a new logic on the basis of one clue. This led him to close "Some Stages of Logical Thought" with a question:

Does not an account of thinking, basing itself on modern scientific procedure, demand a statement in which all the distinctions and terms of thought—judgment, concept, inference, predicate, and copula of judgment, etc., *ad infinitum*—shall be interpreted simply and entirely as distinctive functions or divisions of labor within the doubt-inquiry process? [26]

The promise which was implied in this question remained unfulfilled for almost forty years. The *Logic*, which appeared in 1938, is the work which attempts to demonstrate what was only suggested in 1900 and partially treated in 1903. The success or failure of Dewey's logical project of 1900 can only be judged on the basis of the book he wrote in 1938.

[26] *Ibid.*, p. 219.

CHAPTER ELEVEN

CONCLUSION

The conclusions of this essay can only be the conclusions of a chronicle. The essay has never ranged beyond the purely intellectual aspects of Dewey's development, and therefore it presents no systematic study of the changes which took place in Dewey's environment. The belief that such an extra-intellectual reference is necessary for the explanation of intellectual development is, of course, a hypothesis not to be argued here. Dewey himself has indicated that books were not the only things that made him change his views, and that men and events had a share not to be discounted. The only purpose of such an apologia is to anticipate criticisms which might be leveled by Deweyans themselves. For surely Dewey, more than any of our professional philosophers, has tried to place philosophy's growth in its cultural setting. Even in his first book on a historical problem— the book on Leibniz—Dewey quotes Leibniz' words favorably: "He who knows me only by my writings does not know me"; and he adds himself "These words [are] true, indeed, of every writer." [1] Throughout this essay we have known Dewey only through his writings, but we must add that to know a writer we must at least know his writings, and if this essay is not a Deweyan history of Dewey's philosophy, it is a necessary condition for one.

Throughout the essay I have tried to point up the future significance of many of the things Dewey was saying in the

[1] LNE, p. 1.

eighties and the nineties. In this concluding chapter I wish
to tie together what has been said.

We saw how heavily the influence of George S. Morris
weighed on the early Dewey and how he shaped the earliest
years of Dewey's philosophical development. Morris was
responsible for his turning to Hegel and for the contact
with the neo-Hegelians. Hegel predisposed Dewey against
British empiricism and against Kant—and for the same reason. Both of them committed the sin of constructing dualisms. I cannot stress too heavily the importance of the concept of dualism in Dewey's development. No position, large
or small, that Dewey attacked was not charged at some point
or other with being dualistic. This charge was deemed sufficient to destroy any philosophical claim. We have seen
how this opposition to dualism was originally associated
with a belief in the organic unity of the world, the distinction between organic and mechanical relations, and the
belief that the knowledge-relation is organic. For knowledge
to be an organic relation it is necessary that an organic unity
embrace both the knower and the known object. This is
provided by the theory of the universal consciousness, or
objective mind. It served two progressive purposes. First:
it presented what I have called the "schema" for Dewey's
later naturalism, because it enabled Dewey to conceive of
human and nonhuman things as united in some sense.
Second: the view that there is an absolute mind was the
forerunner of Dewey's belief that all human behavior takes
place in a "cultural matrix."

Soon the impact of evolutionary theory upon Dewey's
thought became stronger. It introduced a new pattern in
his thinking, but it also involved a pattern which was similar to Hegelianism. Darwin, like Hegel, could be used by
someone fighting dualisms, but dualisms of a different variety. He was instrumental in showing that there was something in common between the behavior and the develop-

ment of human beings and nonhuman beings. This reinforced the metaphysical unity between humans and objects which Dewey took over from Hegel. Together, both oppositions to dualism lead to the belief in what Dewey later called "the biological matrix" of all human behavior.

As I have tried to emphasize throughout this essay, the Hegelian and Darwinian approaches were only superficially one. True, they had similarities, but they also had differences, differences which ultimately led Dewey to throw Hegel overboard. The unity achieved by Hegel's universal mind was achieved at a heavy price. It meant that the universe was in some sense constituted by thought before any human mind began to think. On the other hand the force of Darwin's analysis was to portray man and his distinctive capacity—thought—as a product of certain natural forces of adjustment. Adjustment did not mean the reinstatement of some previously existing harmony, and therefore thought was not the deciphering of riddles already solved by an Absolute that kept the answers secret. Thought was an active transformation of a situation, and introduced a new element. It was no playful unearthing of a preëxisting answer, it meant solving problems, finding ways of adjustment which were not known before.

Although the growth of Darwin's influence on Dewey's philosophy meant the surrender of Dewey's idealism, there was one element in Dewey's thought which remained unchanged. He continued to fight strenuously against what he called "formalism." If anything, Darwinism gave more support to this antagonism. Formalism was the formalism of Kant, the scholastics, and Hamilton, all of whom were interested in formal logic. As a result, a kind of indiscriminate assault on formalists and everything they did, set in. It did not matter that some formal logicians never participated in Kantian epistemology. Dewey was sweeping in his attack. So sweeping that in 1891 he rejected all formal logic as useless. It never occurred to Dewey before 1904, I think, that the science of formal logic, as conceived by some logicians, was as epistemologically neutral as any of the other more sedate branches of mathematics. I say 1904, because in that year he wrote an article [2] in which he said that some logicians, like Peirce, were interested in showing that logic was an instrument for arriving at warranted assertions.

This view of formal logic as an instrument became fundamental to Dewey's later views. The *Logic*, when it appeared, could very well include a statement of Dewey's sympathy with Peirce.[3] But this sympathy was relatively recent. Despite the fact that Peirce had taught at Johns Hopkins while Dewey was a graduate student there, Dewey was hardly influenced by him then. Peirce was too much of a formalist for the Hegelian Dewey, and too much of an empiricist for the Dewey who thought in terms of organic relations and absolute minds.[4] Dewey's discovery of Peirce came later, when it was possible for Dewey to see more than intellectual gymnastics in formal logic, when he felt that he could account for it in the framework of a more general theory of inquiry. The later instrumentalism of Dewey marks a period during which any traditional Hegelianism that remained in his thought, remained in spite of his own efforts. The organic unity of idea and fact gave way to the unity of theory and practice; the contradictions between theses and antitheses became conflicting elements in a problematic situation; the Absolute Reason fell before inquiry.

[2] "Notes upon Logical Topics," I, *Journal of Philosophy*, I, 57–62.

[3] See Dewey, *Logic: the Theory of Inquiry*, p. 9n.

[4] Peirce reviewed Dewey's *Studies in Logical Theory*. After referring to what he calls "the German school of logicians," he says: "Prof. Dewey regards himself as radically opposed to the German school, and explains how he is so. We must confess that had he not put so much emphasis upon it, we should hardly have deemed the point of difference so important; but we suppose he must know what his own affiliations are and are not." (*The Nation*, LXXIX (1904), 220.) This remark, however, is followed by a comment in which Peirce expresses his sympathy with Dewey's attempt to develop a natural history of thought.

BIBLIOGRAPHY

For a list of Dewey's writings and writings about him to 1939 see M. H. Thomas, *A Bibliography of John Dewey, 1882–1939*, New York, Columbia University Press, 1939.

For a list of the writings of George S. Morris see R. M. Wenley, *The Life and Work of George Sylvester Morris*, New York, Macmillan, 1917.

Adamson, Robert, A Short History of Logic. Edinburgh, Blackwood, 1911.

Allport, G. W., "Dewey's Individual and Social Psychology," in The Philosophy of John Dewey, Chicago, Northwestern University, 1939, "The Library of Living Philosophers," ed. by P. Schilpp, Vol. I.

Angell, J. R., "The Relations of Structural and Functional Psychology." Chicago, University of Chicago Press, 1903. First Series, Vol. III, of the Decennial Publications of the University of Chicago.

Caird, Edward, "Metaphysics," in Encyclopaedia Britannica, 9th ed., Edinburgh, Black, 1875–1889.

Dewey, Jane M., ed., "Biography of John Dewey," in The Philosophy of John Dewey, Chicago, Northwestern University, 1939. "The Library of Living Philosophers," Vol. I.

Ford, Franklin, Municipal Reform, a Scientific Question. New York, 1903.

Green, T. H., Works of Thomas Hill Green, ed. by R. L. Nettleship. New York, Longmans, 1885–1888.

Hall, G. Stanley, Life and Confessions of a Psychologist. New York, Appleton, 1923.

—— "Notes on Hegel and His Followers," The *Journal of Speculative Philosophy*, XII (Jan., 1878), 93–103.

—— "Philosophy in the United States," *Mind*, IV (Jan., 1879), 89–105.

Huxley, T. H., Evolution and Ethics and Other Essays. New York, Appleton, 1914.

Jones, Henry, A Critical Account of the Philosophy of Lotze. New York, Macmillan, 1895.

Lloyd, Alfred H., Dynamic Idealism. Chicago, McClurg, 1898.

Lotze, H., Logic. 2d ed. Oxford, Clarendon, 1888.

McCosh, James, The Scottish Philosophy. New York, Carter, 1875.

Mansel, H. L., Prolegomena Logica. Oxford, Graham, 1851.

Perry, Ralph Barton, The Thought and Character of William James. Boston, Little, Brown, 1935.

Seth Pringle-Pattison, A., The Development from Kant to Hegel. London, Williams, 1882.

—— The Present Position of the Philosophical Sciences. Edinburgh, Blackwood, 1891.

Seth Pringle-Pattison, A., and R. B. Haldane, eds., Essays in Philosophical Criticism. London, Longmans, 1883.

Venn, John, The Principles of Empirical or Inductive Logic. London, Macmillan, 1889.

INDEX

Abstraction, 115

Act, 110; and consequences of, 111; identity of agent and, 112

Activity, 22, 117

Adamson, Robert, quoted, 72

Advantage, 120

Alexander, Samuel, 100

Allport, G. W., quoted, 107

American philosophy, 1879, 3-11

Applied Psychology (Dewey and Mc-Lellan), 49, 53, 69

Argument, logic of, 70, 88

Aristotle, 18, 60, 90n

Arithmetic, application of evolutionary method in sphere of, 126-133

Bacon, Francis, Morris' treatment of, 14

Bain, Alexander, 4, 29, 30; quoted, 24

Bentham, Jeremy, 23, 24

Berkeley, George, 15, 19, 42

Bibliography, 153 f.

Biology, and concept of organism, 39, 61; influence of, 119, 144; *see also* Evolution

Bosanquet, Bernard, 13, 64, 70, 135, 136

Bourne, Richard Henry Fox, 16

Bradley, F. H., 64, 70, 71, 100, 113, 135, 136

British philosophy, 13, 91; Dewey's attitude toward, 4, 36, 39, 60, 91, 150; late 19th century books on logic, 64; *see also* Empiricism

British Thought and Thinkers (Morris), 12, 13-25, 26

Burnham, W. H., 38

Caird, Edward, 5, 6, 9, 13, 34, 35, 41, 46n, 47, 49, 55, 64, 99, 100, 104, 148

Cattell, J. Mackeen, 38

Classification, unity of, 115, 116

Class-membership, 116

Coherence theory of truth, 79

Colleges and universities, status of philosophy during Dewey's student years, 3, 7; Johns Hopkins and its department of philosophy in 1882, 6-11

Concept, 65, 69

Conception, 75, 78

Conflict, as origin of thought, 81; evolutionary significance of, 120; Deweyan view, 121; as law of cosmic process, 122

Consciousness, British empiricists' concept of, 19, 21; universal, 31, 43-47, 50 ff., 58, 97, 150; individual, 46, 51, 55, 97; theory of "two minds," 50 ff., 97; intelligence, 51, 102, 118n, 120; objective, 57, 150

Constitutive thought, 138, 140, 147

Constructivist theory of mathematical definitions, 67

Correspondence theory of truth, 79

Cosmic process, law of, 122 ff.

Counting and measuring, 129

Critical Account of the Philosophy of Lotze (Jones), 135

Critical Philosophy of Immanuel Kant, The (Caird), 6, 100

Cultural setting and philosophy, 149

D'Arcy, C. F., 107

Darwinism, 40, 61, 121, 150, 151; *see also* Evolution

Deductive Logic (Stock), 86

Descartes, René, 35, 62

Dewey, Jane, biographical sketch by, 4n, 100; quoted, 38

Dewey, John, student years and influences, 3-9; Jane Dewey's biographical sketch of, 4n, 100; back-

Dewey, John (*Continued*)
ground of Scottish philosophy, 4; attitude toward empiricism, 4, 36, 39 ff., 60, 91, 150; proclaimed unity of morals and theology, 5; Morris' influence on, 7, 9, 11, 12, 18, 20, 27, 30, 32, 34, 59, 150; Peirce's, 7, 11, 152; relations with Hall, 8, 9, 34, 38; interest in experimental psychology, 8, 37-41; at University of Michigan, 10, 98; influences that led him to Hegel, 13, 150 (*see also* Hegel, G. W. F.); beginning of his crusade against the spectator theory of knowledge, 18; of his activism, 22, 27; choice of "experimentalism" as a name for his philosophy, 29*n*, 83; concepts influencing his early work, 31; sources for his attack on dualism, 32; attempt to state the relation between idealism and psychology, 34-48; first paper on Kant, and concern with philosophic method, 34, 35-37, 121; articles in *Mind*, 35, 41, 47, 55, 59, 64; praise of Hegel, 37, 93; similarity of approach between Hegel and biology, paved way for second period of career, 40; opposition to formal logic, 40 f., 64, 86, 151; attempt to defend the thesis that philosophy was psychology, 42; first three books, 49-63; definitions of psychology, 49, 52; two fundamental divisions in early psychology of, 53*n*; rejected theory of "two minds" when he later surrendered idealist conception of thought, 55; ambivalence in all aspects of early thought, 56; qualities in early thought which flow from his "two minds," 57; the logic of empiricism, 64-78; first logical writings, 65, 69; review and criticism of Venn's *Principles of . . . Logic*, 69, 73-78; early writings merely the beginnings of doctrine as known today, 69; pragmatist elements in earliest thought of, 69, 99; position taken in "The Logic of Verification," 79-95; definite departure from idealistic logic, 79; veering from Hegel, 85; first lengthy critique of formal logic, 86; last great defense of Hegel, 92-94; defensive about acceptance of transcendental logic, 92; Deweyan logic reached as result of work in other fields, 95; two extended studies of ethical idealism, 96-98; most explicit criticisms of idealism first appeared in his discussion of ethical questions, 96; book on, and course in, ethics, evidence shifting outlook, 98 f.; instrumentalist ideas begin to appear in philosophy of, 99; the impending break with idealism, 100 ff.; influence of Franklin Ford, 100-102, 103; beginning of crusade for application of intelligence in social affairs, 102; influence of Green, 104, 113; attack on Green, 104-106; criticism of James, 106; as known at present makes his appearance at last, in the *Syllabus*, 109; book in which experimentalism first appears, 110; continuity between his idealism and experimentalism, 110, 111; experimental idealism as name for the philosophy accepted at transitional point in his history, 112; connection with Mead; 114; resemblances between early ideas of, and the work of Lloyd, 114-119; contact with evolutionary thought, 119; tendency to draw upon psychology, sociology, biology, 120; arrival at Deweyan view of conflict, 121; criticism of Huxley's "Evolution and Ethics" his most vigorous defense of evolutionary thought, 121-125; first attempt to deal with a formal concept, 126; evolutionary method applied in the *Psychology of Number*, 126; Fine's review of the book, 127-131; reply, 131-133; first detailed expression of his new ideas in the *Studies in Logical Theory*, 134-148; attitude toward Lotze, 135-148 *passim;* reasons for diverging from idealism, 138; op-

position to a nongenetic approach in logic, 143; first lengthy statement of position later to become instrumentalism, 147; first paper criticizing transcendental logic, 147; an ex-idealist, 148; influences in development of, summarized, 149 ff.; tried to place philosophy's growth in its cultural setting, 149; importance of his constant opposition to dualism, 150; influence of Darwinism upon, summarized, 151; overthrow of Hegel, 151; view of formal logic as an instrument, 152

Donaldson, H. H., 38

Dualism, Morris' analysis, 31; beginnings of Dewey's attack on, 32; an extreme form of anti-dualism, 118n; importance of concept of, in Dewey's development, 150

Dynamic Idealism (Lloyd), 113-119

Ego, 106

Elementary Lessons in Logic (Jevons), 86, 88

Emotion, 121n

"Empirical Survey of Empiricisms, An" (Dewey), 29n

Empiricism, leading British exponents of, 4; Dewey's attitude toward, 4, 36, 39, 41, 60, 91, 150; reaction against, 13; Morris' opposition to, 13, 29 ff.; logic of, 64-78, 90

Essays in Philosophical Criticism, 13, 34, 35

Ethical idealism, *see* Idealism

Ethical Studies (Bradley), 100

Ethics, courses at Michigan, 98; Dewey's first writings on, 98 ff.; and evolution, 121-125; sympathy and coöperation the law of, 122

"Ethics and Physical Science" (Dewey), 96, 98

"Ethics of Democracy, The" (Dewey), 96, 98

Evolution, impact upon Dewey's thought, 40, 61, 150; and idealism, 109-125; and immediate truths, 119; and conflict, 120 f.; and ethics, 121-125; application of method of, in the sphere of number, 126-133; identification of "the natural history of thought" and logic, 144 ff.

"Evolution and Ethics" (Dewey), 121-125

"Evolution and Ethics" (Huxley), 121-125

"Existence of the World as a Logical Problem, The" (Dewey), 30n

Experience, 20, 30, 42

Experimental idealism, 110-113

Experimentalism, Dewey's choice of, as name for his philosophy, 29n, 83, 111; first book showing signs of, 110; continuity between Dewey's idealism and, 111

Experimental psychology, 8, 37-41

Facts, 98; individual, 50, 51; universal, 51; and ideas, 79, 80 ff.

Fine, H. B., review of the *Psychology of Number*, 127-131; Dewey's reply, 131-133

Fischer, Kuno, 71

"Fixation of Belief, The" (Peirce), 8

Ford, Franklin, and his influence on Dewey, 100-102, 103

Formal logic, *see* Logic

Frege, G., analysis of concept of number, 126, 131, 133

"From Absolutism to Experimentalism" (Dewey), 12

"German Philosophic Classics for English Readers and Students," 26

German philosophy, Morris' enthusiasm for, 13; books to spread truth about, 26, 49, 59

Gilman, Daniel Coit, 6; an anti-metaphysician, 7; rift with Morris, 9

Green, Thomas Hill, 9, 25, 32, 41, 49, 64, 96, 97, 99, 100, 124, 148; reconciliation of science and religion, 5; *Introduction* to Hume, 13; logic and logicians, 70, 86n, 87; influence on Dewey, 104, 113; doctrine of the self criticized, 104-106; conception of self-realization, 112, 113

Haldanes, R. B., 13

Hall, G. Stanley, 4, 6, 9; quoted, 3, 10; reputation and achievements, 8; relations with Dewey, 8, 34, 38; attack on Dewey's Hegelianism, 9; propagandist for experimental psychology: students of, 38

Hamilton, Sir William, 4, 19, 30, 64, 71, 72, 73, 87; Morris' treatment of, 20, 22 f.; criticisms of the formal logic of, 86-88

Harrison, Frederic, 83n

Hartwell, E. M., 38

Hegel, G. W. F., 9, 13, 32, 40, 49, 56, 60, 64, 85, 96, 98, 121, 135, 151; prominent opponents of Hegelianism, 8; Morris came to Kant through, 13; completes Kant, 37; conception of objective mind, 58; Dewey veering from, 85; his last great defense of, 92-94; the "quintessence of the scientific spirit," 93; early influence upon Dewey, 150; causes of Dewey's disagreement with, 151

Hegel's Philosophy of the State and of History (Morris), 12

Hobbes, Thomas, 15

"How Do Concepts Arise from Percepts" (Dewey), 66n

"How to Make Our Ideas Clear" (Peirce), 8

How We Think (Dewey), 77n

Hume, David, 15, 19, 42, 60; Green's Introduction to, 13

Huxley, Thomas, 83n; "Evolution and Ethics," 121-125

Hyslop, James H., 38

Idealism, British, 13; and the new psychology, 34-48; Kant and the philosophic method, 35-37; philosophy and psychology, 41-48; two key doctrines of idealistic psychology, 54; most explicit criticisms of, 96; Dewey's two extended studies of ethical idealism, 96-98; and impending break with it, 98-108; evolution and, 109-125; experimental, 110-113 (see also Experimentalism); Lloyd's Dynamic Idealism,

113-119; relation between Lotze and idealist logic, 135 ff.; Dewey's reasons for diverging from, 138; his break with, 147

Ideas, innate, 17; and objects, 74, 76; and facts, 79, 80 ff.; as plans, 119

Image, 66

Immediate knowledge, 119

Impulsive acts, 112

Inductive logic, see Logic

Inference, 77, 89

Innate ideas, 17

Instrumentalism, most significant signs begin to appear, 99; first lengthy statement of position later to become, 147

Instrumental logic, 41; Lotze and, 134-148

Intelligence, 51, 102, 118n, 120; social function, 102; see also Consciousness; Thought

Introspection, 57, 58

"Is Logic a Dualistic Science?" (Dewey), 69

James, William, 8, 99, 100, 113, 118, 134; Dewey's criticism of, 106; quoted, 107

Jastrow, Joseph, 38

Jevons, William Stanley, 70, 86, 88, 91; critique of the logic of, 88-91

Johns Hopkins University, founded: emphasis on graduate study, 6; department of philosophy, 7-11

Jones, Henry, attack on Lotze, 135-137

Kant, Immanuel, 18, 56, 60, 92, 99, 104, 150; Morris came to, through Hegel, 13; influence on Morris, 20; Morris' critique of, 20-22; his book on Kant's Critique of Pure Reason, 26, 59; Dewey's first paper on, 34, 35-37, 121; Green really a Kantian? 105

"Kant and Philosophic Method" (Dewey), 34

Kant's Critique of Pure Reason (Morris), 12, 26, 59

Kidd, Benjamin, 120

Knowledge, 42 ff.; spectator theory

of, 15; Morris' analysis of knowledge-situation, 31; defined, 51; discussion of, in the *Psychology*, 53 ff.; two key doctrines of Dewey's theory, 54; and perception, 74, 78; changes in conception of, 147; as organic relation, 150

Lectures on Logic (Green), 71
Leibniz, Gottfried Wilhelm von, 60, 94, 119; Dewey's book on, 8, 26, 49, 59-63, 116; the Locke-Leibniz debate, 17, 62; concept of organism, 61
Leibniz's New Essays concerning the Human Understanding (Dewey), 8, 26, 49, 59-63, 116
Lloyd, Alfred, 134; *Dynamic Idealism*, 113-119
Locke, John, 17, 42, 60, 62, 73, 91; Morris' attack on, 15-18
Logic, Dewey's opposition to formal, 40, 64, 151; instrumental, 41; of empiricism, 64-78, 91; Dewey's earliest writings on, 65, 69; Seth's comments, 84n; Dewey's first lengthy critique of formal, 86; inductive, is scientific, 92; Dewey's acceptance and defense of, transcendental, 92; Dewey on formal, inductive, and transcendental, 94; new, or Deweyan, offered, 95; Lotze and instrumental logic, 134-148; general problem of theory, 139; pure, 140-142; applied, 141, 142; identification of, with "the natural history of thought," 142-148; Dewey's first paper criticizing transcendental, 147; view of formal, as an instrument, 152
Logic (Bosanquet), 64
Logic (Dewey), 111, 144, 148, 152
"Logic of Verification, The" (Dewey), 79-95
Logic (Lotze), 64, 140
Logicians, classification of, 70
Logic of J. S. Mill, The (Green), 71
Logic of the Formal Logicians, The (Green), 71
Lotze, Rudolf H., 64, 70; Dewey's

attitude toward, 135-148 *passim;* Jones' attack on, 135-137
Luria, A. R., 121n

McCosh, James, 3, 4, 5, 6
McLellan, J. A., and Dewey, John, 49, 126
Maine, Sir Henry, 98
Mansel, H. L., 71, 72, 87; criticisms of the formal logic of, 86-88, 90
Mathematical definitions, constructivist theory, 67
Mead, George Herbert, 114, 134
Measuring and counting, 129
Michigan, University of, 10, 98
Mill, James, 23, 73
Mill, John Stuart, 4, 19, 30, 64, 71, 72, 91, 135, 148; Morris' treatment of, 23 f.
Mind, Dewey's articles in, 35, 41, 47, 55, 59, 64
Mind, universal and individual, 50 ff., 97; *see also* Consciousness
Moral Order and Progress (Alexander), 100
Morals, relation between philosophy, theology and, 5
Morris, George Sylvester, 6, 12-33, 73, 96, 116, 148; belief in the relation between philosophy, morals, and theology, 5; at Johns Hopkins, 6, 7, 12 ff.; rift with its president, 9 f.; achievements, 7, 12; influence on Dewey, 7, 9, 11, 12, 18, 20, 27, 30, 32, 34, 59, 150; major interest, 12; dislike of British thought, 12, 13; preference for German thought, 12, 26; philosophers attacked or approved in his *British Thought and Thinkers,* 13-25; critiques of Kant, 20-22, 26; book on Kant, 26, 59; works presenting his own philosophy, 26-32; books to spread truth about German philosophy, 26, 49, 59; paper summarizing his whole philosophy, 27 ff.
Motora, Y., 38

Naturalism, 45
Nelson, J., 38
Nettleship, Richard, 71

"New Psychology, The" (Dewey), 34, 39

Norm, theory of, 110, 125

Number, application of evolutionary method in sphere of, 126-133; origin and nature, 128

Object, knowledge of, 74 ff.

Objective mind, theory of, 57, 150; *see also* Consciousness

Object-subject relation, 31, 37, 45

Optimism, 39

Organicism, concept of, 39, 61, 137; gives way to traces of instrumentalism, 99

Organic unity, concept of, 111

Organic relations, 31 f.

Organization, unity of, 116

Our Knowledge of the External World (Russell), 30n

Outlines of a Critical Theory of Ethics (Dewey), 70, 98 ff., 109, 110, 111

Patrick, G. W. T., 38

Peirce, Charles, 6, 9, 129n; early neglect of, 3, 8n; reputation and achievements, 7; Dewey's attitude toward, 7, 11, 152

Percept, 66

Perception, 74, 78

Philosophical Discussions (Wright), 3

Philosophy, conditions during Dewey's student years, 3-11; Scottish, 3, 4-6; at Johns Hopkins university, 7-11; British, condemned by Morris, 12 ff.; problem of relation between psychology and, 15, 35, 41-48; distinction between science and, 25; Morris' division of epochal works in history of, 59

Philosophy and Christianity (Morris), 5

"Philosophy and Its Specific Problems" (Morris), 27

Philosophy of John Dewey, The (ed. by P. Schilpp), 4n

Physical science, 27 ff.; *see also* Science

Physiological Psychology (Wundt), 38

Plato, 60

Pragmatist elements in early thought of Dewey, 69, 99

"Present Position of Logical Theory, The" (Dewey), 99, 103

"Present Position of the Philosophical Sciences, The" (Seth), 84n

Principles of Empirical or Inductive Logic (Venn), 69, 73

Principles of Logic (Bradley), 64, 71

Principles of Science (Jevons), 91

Pringle-Pattison (Andrew Seth), 13, 36, 84n

Prolegomena Logica (Mansel), 88, 90

Prolegomena to Ethics (Green), 100

Propositions arrived at inferentially, 77

Psychic Factors of Civilization, The (Ward), 120

"Psychological Standpoint, The" (Dewey), 35, 42, 50, 52, 55

Psychology, experimental, 8, 37-41; problem of relation between philosophy and, 15, 35, 41-48; distinction between empirical and rational, 16; idealism and the new psychology, 34-48; Kant and the philosophic method, 35-37; defined, 49, 52; two fundamental divisions in Dewey's early, 53n; two key doctrines of idealistic, 54; from ethical idealism to social psychology, 96-108; *see also* Idealism

Psychology (Dewey), 9, 34, 38, 48, 49-59, 65, 66n, 78, 106, 107, 119, 147

"Psychology as Philosophic Method" (Dewey), 35

Psychology of Number, The (Dewey and McLellan), 126-133

Realism, Scottish, 6

Reason and its material, 36

Reid, Thomas, 4

Relation, dynamic, 114 ff.

Relations, mechanical and organic, 31

Religion, reconciliation of science and, 5

Renan, Ernest, 102
Robertson, J. Croom, 15
Russell, Bertrand, 30, 127

Sanford, E. C., 38
Scholastics, 91, 92
Science, reconciliation of religion and, 5; distinction between philosophy and, 25; physical, 27 ff.; logic of, 70; attempts to formulate a methodology of, 83, 91 f.; Hegel the quintessence of the scientific spirit, 93; social function, 103
Scottish philosophy, 3, 4-6
Self, doctrine of, 104; dynamic relation, 114
Self-consciousness, 49, 55n
Self-realization, 106, 112, 113, 124
"Self-Realization as the Moral Ideal" (Dewey), 106
Sensations, 43, 44, 74; defined, 53; are not knowledge, 54
Seth (Pringle-Pattison) Andrew, 13, 36, 84n
Short Study of Ethics, A (D'Arcy), 107
Sign, concept of, 54
Sigwart, C., 70, 71
Social Evolution (Kidd), 120
Social function, of intelligence, 102; of science, 103
Social Philosophy of Comte (Caird), 100
Social psychology, from ethical idealism to, 96-108
"Social Psychology" (Dewey), 120
Social sciences, emphasis upon, 58
"Some Stages of Logical Thought" (Dewey), 94, 147, 148
Spencer, Herbert, 4, 19, 27; Morris' treatment of, 25; argument against, 97
Stewart, Dugald, 4
Stock, St. George, 86
Struggle, see Conflict

Studies in Logical Theory (Dewey), 56, 109, 111, 125, 134-148, 152n
Study of Ethics, The: a Syllabus (Dewey), 96, 107, 109, 110, 114, 119, 123
Subject-object relation, 31, 37, 45
Swift, M. I., 38
Syllabus, see Study of Ethics

Tension, see Conflict
Theology, relation between philosophy, morals and, 5
Theory, 82
"Theory of Emotion, The" (Dewey), 121n
Thought and thinking, 36, 65; intelligence, 51, 102, 118n, 120; defined, 65; two methods of, 70; conflict and tension essential to, 81, 121, 122; relation between fact and, 84; conception of, at bottom of formal logic, 86 ff.; is universal, 118n; reality and, 135; constitutive, 138, 140, 147; derivative and secondary, 140; pure logic devoted to, 140; identification of logic and "the natural history of thought," 142-148
Torrey, H. A. P., 4
Transcendental logic, 92, 94, 147

Ueberweg, Friedrich, 71; Morris' translation of his history of philosophy, 12
Universities, see Colleges and universities

Venn, John, logic of, 69, 70, 73-78 passim, 91
Verification, logic of, 79-95

Ward, Lester, 120
Wenley, R. M., 7, 9
Wordsworth, William, 24
Wright, Chauncey, 3
Wundt, Wilhelm, 35, 38, 41, 70